Advanced Shell Script Programming

For Business Continuity and Data Center Automation

Part 1: The Template

By
Dana French

Note to Reader: If you are reading this book on a portable device, it will be best viewed in Landscape mode.

Contents

Forward

The materials presented in this book are at the forefront of a new mentality in Information Technology Management. This mentality is a movement away from the interactive requirements of data center management tools of the past, and toward a totally automated environment. This automation includes not only the deployment and configuration of new and existing systems, but the ability to generate documentation instead of writing it. This automated documentation is generated by the systems themselves and used for system support, maintenance, disaster recovery, audit compliance and response, training, and other purposes. The point is to eliminate the latency between system changes, and documentation updates, the goal being a greater assurance of business continuity.

Much of the material in this book is technical in nature, but it is always presented with an eye toward business continuity. This is to reinforce the primary objective of this book, which is the implementation of data center automation as a mechanism of achieving business continuity.

Introduction

Do you remember when you were in school and the classes you were taking had titles such as "Introduction to this...", "Basic Principles of that..."? You probably never had a course, class, or book whose title began with "Advanced..."? Well, guess what, today is the day!

Please be aware the title of this book does not begin with "Advanced..." for no reason or just to draw attention to itself. This is not a book for beginners to shell scripting. This book assumes you are already an accomplished writer of shell scripts, and does not cover the basics or syntax. This book discusses advanced techniques and methodologies. To determine if this book is for you ask yourself the following questions:

- Do I know the difference between shell built-in commands and UNIX commands?

- Do I use shell script functions regularly in my scripts?

- Do I use the "getopts" function regularly in scripts?

- Do I use "traps" in my scripts?

- Do I know what "positional parameters" are and how to use them?

- Do I know what "variable operators" are and how to use them?

- Do I know the difference between math operators and string comparison operators?

If you answered "yes" to all of the above questions, then continue reading, you passed the test, and you are ready. But be aware that answering "yes" to the above questions does not mean you are familiar with the contents of this book. Most of the topics in the question list above, will be covered in the first couple of chapters when you build a template shell script. And most people reading this book will have difficulty understanding the first few chapters, even if they are accomplished script writers.

The topics discussed in this book will include advanced techniques for writing shell scripts, automated documentation, managing function libraries, coding conventions, and several other techniques oriented around enhancing your organizations business continuity capabilities. In fact, by the end of this book, the reader should realize this is actually an exercise in implementing Business Continuity using Advanced Shell Scripting to accomplish the task.

Chapter 1: Business Continuity thru Data Center Automation

The entire future of any organization is dependent upon the system administrator's ability to implement business continuity (BC) plans and actions. BC incorporates a wide range of technologies under numerous subject matters, including data center automation. In fact, automation is a key driving force toward profitability in a modern data center. Your competitors are hard at work attempting to reduce costs and increase performance, reliability, and consistency by investing in data center automation. If your competitors achieve automation first, you and your business will be left behind struggling to play "catch-up". If you work in a for-profit environment, then your data center operational goals must be oriented around automation. Whether this automation utilizes local resources, cloud resources, or a hybrid combination of both is irrelevant. The goal must be automation over all resources, regardless of where they may exist. And the most important thing to know about automation is:

Data center automation is largely performed by shell scripts.

This means that system administrators must be expert shell scripters, not competent, not adequate, they must be experts. Virtually anyone can write a basic shell script, it is not difficult. The difficulty lies in translating automation procedures into step-by-step system commands, and this takes expert level shell scripting.

In order to understand the importance of shell scripting in today's modern data center environment, it is necessary to define some of the concepts that will be used throughout this book.

- **Business Continuity** – *policies, guidelines, standards, procedures*
- **Data Center Automation** – *The strength of Unix / Linux*
- **Shell Scripting** – *The mechanism of Automation*

The greatest attribute of UNIX and Linux is the ability to automate tasks, processes, and functions. The mechanism by which this automation occurs, normally begins with, or consists entirely of, is a shell script. To be really good at automation, requires system administrators to be really good at shell scripting. To be an expert at automation requires expert shell scripting. Basic knowledge of shell scripting will only achieve basic automation (something your competitors can easily do).

This series of books is intended to provide a system administrator (who has basic knowledge of shell programming) with advanced shell scripting capabilities such that they will be able to automate any task they wish to perform. These tasks include automated documentation, code generators, process scheduling, high availability fail overs, disaster recovery, etc. The first book of this series will focus on:

Part One: The Template

- Shell Script Functions and Function Libraries

- Multi-Shell Coding

- Automated Documentation

- Introduction to Local or Remote Execution Coding

This series of books does not discuss basic or introductory techniques, features, or concepts. These books contain "Advanced" concepts and are not meant for the novice or beginner in Shell Programming.

This first book will concentrate on a standardized shell scripting template that can be used to create every new shell script. It will provide a starting point at which the advanced shell programmer can begin, without having to start from zero every time. The template utilizes several functions, techniques, and features which can be customized to accommodate any requirement.

Numerous concepts and techniques will be discussed in a series of progressive improvements to the basic template. These progressive improvements will start with a discussion of beginning every script as a shell script function, and how to determine what type of function should be defined. The next discussion will describe the shell function library, how to create and reference functions from the library.

The standardized shell script template will include the following parts and components:

- Usage Message

- Dynamic Configuration

- Signal Traps

- Command Line Option Processing

- Embedded Documentation

- Standardized Variables

  ○ TRUE

  ○ FALSE

  ○ VERBOSE

  ○ VERYVERB

The discussion of standardized shell script components will be followed by a discussion of function libraries and how to implement them in Korn Shell, Bash, and Z-Shell. Even though the functions in the library will be the same between the various shells, the implementation of the function libraries will be different.

Once the concept of functions and function libraries is complete, we will then discuss how to write shell code so that it is portable and executable between varieties of shell script interpreters, specifically:

- Korn Shell

- Bash

- Z-Shell

Writing portable code will require utilizing specific techniques to generalize certain shell commands, such as I/O commands, looping commands, and others. These techniques serve to generalize the shell code so that it is executable across numerous shell interpreters without code changes.

One of the advanced programming techniques to be discussed will be "Automated Documentation". In order to provide Data Center Automation, any new shell scripts (or any other program) should be created as "functions" and have the ability to **self-document.** This means that each function should have the ability to create its own documentation using self-generated usage messages and embedded comments. The automated documentation should be compatible with a wide variety of formats, therefore the "Grutatxt" markup technique will be recommended and outlined (Grutatxt will be explained later). This means the embedded comments in each shell script should be in the Grutatxt markup format. These comments can then be extracted from each function and formatted for any purpose, such as for MediaWiki or other documentation server. This automation technique will be detailed and explained in a later chapter.

Another technique to be discuss will be referred to as "Local/Remote Command Execution". This technique permits the shell programmer to write scripts that dynamically determine whether to execute commands on the local system, or on a remote system using a command execution tool such as "ssh". The technique involves writing the shell code in such a way that it becomes transparent to the shell script programmer whether the command is being executed locally or remote, as well as capturing the results.

Obviously if a command is executed remotely, there is additional information required such as the remote system name, login information, network ports, etc. This technique allows the script user to specify this information on the command line, and provides a transparent mechanism for using this information within the script. The command execution line within the script determines whether to perform the command locally or remotely based on the information provided by the user. This description seems like the technique would simply be to require an "if" statement to make this decision for each command to be executed, but as you will see it is really more of a programming style than an "if" statement decision. More on this technique in later chapters.

This Local/Remote technique can be used with automation functions to perform installation and configuration of software, data changes, verification of components, etc. This technique is useful to consolidate these types of functions into a single function that can automatically detect where to perform the target commands.

At this point you may be asking why is this chapter titled "Business Continuity thru Data Center Automation?" What does Data Center Automation have to do with Business Continuity? To explain this, let's first define the term "Business Continuity".

Business Continuity is a pre-defined methodology of conducting day-to-day business.

Business Continuity permeates all aspects of conducting business from Sales and Marketing to Human Resources, from Transportation to Warehousing, from the IT department to the executive suite, and everything in between.

Many people confuse Business Continuity with Disaster Recovery, but they are different.

Disaster Recovery is a short term project plan that is implemented in the event of a disaster.

Whereas;

Business Continuity is a methodology of conducting day-to-day activities by every person in an organization, in every aspect of their job. The foundation of Business Continuity is:

Policies:

Those things mandated by management of an organization that will always be performed according to a preset design plan, and supporting all business functions within an organization.

Guidelines:

Those things which are recommended to be performed according to a preset design plan. However depending upon the needs and requirements of the target business function, these items may or may not be performed, or may be altered during implementations.

Standards:

Consists of the technical specifications for the implementation of all business functions, and are derived from the Policies and Guidelines

Procedures:

The step-by-step instructions for the implementation of organizational Standards as applied to any business function.

Data Center Automation is the actual implementation of Business Continuity Procedures.

The reader should realize from this discussion of Business Continuity, that data center automation is the result of a well thought out and designed environment. It requires conscience knowledge of every step-by-step execution of commands to perform any task. Every single command needed to perform a task must be known and documented in order for any task to be automated. Not only does every single step-by-step command need to be accounted for, but the documentation, auditing, training, and support requirements must also be included for the automation to be complete.

The point is that Data Center Automation is not simple.

There is much, much more to Data Center Automation than writing a few scripts. It requires planning and commitment from everyone in the organization, including management. Your automation plan should include consideration of:

- Change Control

- Service Level Agreements

- Automated Documentation

- Help Desk

- Support Notification

- Personnel Training

- On-boarding of new Personnel

- Outsourcing

- Facilities / Resource Utilization

- Infrastructure

- Intellectual Property

- Turnover and loss of knowledge base

- Regulatory and Audit Compliance

- Information availability and integrity

- Recoverability of business functions

- Customer and Supplier confidence

So you may ask again "What does Business Continuity have to do with Data Center Automation?" And the answer is, *everything*.

If your goal is Data Center Automation, then you have embarked upon a difficult, but very rewarding task.

> **Achieving data center automation is much like the old joke "How do you eat an elephant?" - "One bite at a time."**

As a first bite of the data center automation elephant, define the foundations of your Business Continuity plan, i.e., policies, guidelines, standards, and procedures. And since the topic of this book is Advanced Shell Scripting Techniques, first concentrate on those policies, guidelines, standards, and procedures associated with shell scripting.

What would these foundations look like? Here are some examples:

Shell Scripting Policies

> Mandatory conformance with your organizations shell scripting style guide. (You will need to write/adopt a shell scripting style guide after reading this book.)

Shell Scripting Guidelines

> Repeatable tasks will be written as reusable functions and called from a function library.

(You will need to create function library(s) after reading this book.)

Shell Scripting Standards

Use templates to create all shell scripts (This book will provide you with these templates.)

Shell Scripting Procedures

This will be the implementation of your shell scripts that you create after reading this book.

One last thought for this first chapter: An Advanced Shell Script Programmer must also be an expert user of an advanced text editor such as emacs, vi, or other. And as a reference point, "notepad" is NOT an advanced text editor.

The remainder of this book focuses on several shell script templates which will provide the BC foundation discussed in this chapter. And remember, the key to success in Data Center Automation is to take small bites.

Chapter 2: The Basic Template

We will begin with a basic template that utilizes numerous advanced shell scripting techniques to achieve Data Center Automation (DCA) and comply with Business Continuity (BC) requirements. Each chapter is organized in such a way as to identify the BC foundations and DCA techniques at the beginning of each chapter.

This first Basic template will introduce and illustrate the following Business Continuity principles.

Business Continuity Foundations

- Shell Scripting Policies
    - o Reusable tasks written as functions
    - o Embedded documentation
- Shell Scripting Guidelines
    - o Korn Shell 93 or Bash
    - o Usage message
    - o Dynamic configuration
    - o Command line option processing using "getopts"
- Shell Scripting Standards
    - o Grutatxt markup for embedded comments
- Shell Scripting Procedures
    - o ksh93 Function
    - o Traps
    - o Variable typesets
    - o Local variables in functions
    - o Embedded status reporting

In this chapter we will examine the Basic template in sections. The complete source code of the Basic template is available in Appendix A.

You will want to copy this Basic template to a file on your UNIX/Linux/Cygwin desktop for reference and testing.

The first thing to notice about the Basic template is the overall structure. The script is organized as a standalone shell script, divided into several functions. It contains a documentation section, a configuration section, a command line option processing section, an error processing section, and finally the main body of the script. We will identify and examine each of these sections in detail to understand how they work together to achieve BC and DCA.

It is recommended that shell scripts be written as functions. The standalone portion of the shell script should simply define the required global variables needed to perform some task, and then make external calls to shell script functions that exist in one or more function libraries. This shell script programming policy has numerous benefits to the organization:

- Centralized location of code

- Repeatable and reusable code

- Standardized mechanisms for common tasks

- Enables Code auditing and style guides

- Standardized Training

- Standardized Documentation

- Centralized and transferable knowledge base for:

    ○ On-boarding

    ○ Support

    ○ Maintenance

    ○ Testing/Development

    ○ Training

During the discussion of the templates provided in this book, several different types of users will be described. It is important to understand the difference between these users:

- **Function programmer:** This is a user that is writing a shell script function to be included in a function library.

- **Script programmer:** This is a user that is writing a shell script and/or function which calls external functions from one or more shell script libraries.

- **Script User:** This user is executing shell scripts from the command line or scheduling them to be executed.

The functions defined in this first Basic template include the following:

- usagemsg_my_template01_ksh93

  - Korn Shell Function

  - Displays a usage message to standard output

- configure_my_template01_ksh93

  - POSIX Function

  - Dynamic configuration of the template function

- my_template01_ksh93

  - Korn Shell Function

  - Main body of the shell scripting

The usage message function displays instructions for executing the shell script. It provides a description of the function, lists command line options, syntax, and any other information the function programmer thinks is relevant to the script programmer.

```
##################################################
function usagemsg_my_template01_k93 {
  print "
Program: my_template01_k93

Place a brief description ( < 255 chars ) of your shell
function here.

Usage: ${1##*/} [-?vV]

  Where:
    -v = Verbose mode - displays my_template01_k93 function info
    -V = Very Verbose Mode - debug output displayed
    -? = Help - display this message

Author: Your Name (YourEmail@address.com)
\"AutoContent\" enabled
"
```

```
}
##################################################
```

In this template usage message function, only a couple of command line options are shown as examples. Your usage message functions should contain and describe all of the options relevant to the execution of your shell scripts. In this example, the command line options displayed are:

- -v: Display verbose status messages as specified by the function programmer

- -V: Display very verbose messaging, which turns on the X-Trace mode shell option. This is equivalent of running the "set -x" command. If you are unfamiliar with X-Trace mode, you will want to look this up in a shell syntax manual.

The format of the text in the usage message may conform to any existing standard already adopted or in use by your organization. The example message format shown in these templates resembles the UNIX "man" page format, but the reader should modify this to fit their own needs and organizational requirements.

Every function should have an associated usage message function to provide instructions and documentation of the function.

The next section of interest from the Basic template is a documentation area.

```
##################################################
####
#### Description:
####
#### Place a full text description of your shell function here.
####
#### Assumptions:
####
#### Provide a list of assumptions your shell function makes,
#### with a description of each assumption.
####
#### Dependencies:
####
#### Provide a list of dependencies your shell function has,
#### with a description of each dependency.
####
#### Products:
####
#### Provide a list of output your shell function produces,
#### with a description of each product.
####
#### Configured Usage:
####
#### Describe how your shell function should be used.
####
#### Details:
```

```
####
#### Place nothing here, the details are your shell function.
####
#################################################
```

Each new shell script function should have a similar documentation section embedded within the function. This documentation section should provide as a minimum, the following information:

- Description: A short description of the purpose of the function.

- Assumptions: A list of assumptions that are made when executing this function.

- Dependencies: A list of dependencies this function has in order execute properly. This may include a list of external programs, utilities, or other functions.

- Products: A description of the output produced by the execution of this function.

- Configured Usage: A description of how to execute this function and why, maybe include an example command line.

NOTE: Each line of this documentation section begins with 4 #'s followed by a space. In regular expression syntax: "^#### ". This is a text markup indicator that is used to identify embedded comments within the functions and shell script, and it will be automatically processed to generate documentation. This will be discussed in much greater detail in later chapters, but it is sufficient for now to simply understand this text markup indicates embedded documentation. Also understand this concept is an important part of Data Center Automation as well as Business Continuity.

The next section of the Basic template contains a POSIX function named "configure_my_template_k93".

```
#################################################
configure_my_template01_k93()
{
####
#### Notice this function is a POSIX function so that it can see local
#### and global variables from calling functions and scripts.
####
#### Configuration parameters can be stored in a file and
#### this script can be dynamically reconfigured by sending
#### the running script a HUP signal using the kill command.
####
#### Configuration variables can be defined in the configuration file using
```

```
#### the same syntax as defining a shell variable, e.g.: VARIABLE="value"

CFILE=~/.my_template01_k93.conf

(( VERBOSE == TRUE )) && print -- "# Configuration File: ${CFILE}"

if [[ -f ${CFILE} ]]
then
    (( VERBOSE == TRUE )) && cat ${CFILE}
    . ${CFILE}
fi

return 0
}
###################################################
```

The purpose of this section of the script is to provide a dynamic mechanism of configuring the shell script function. It executes a configuration file which is assumed to also contain shell code. Usually this file contains shell variable definitions, however it may contain any shell code desired, including references to outside functions, applications, or utilities.

Notice this configuration function is defined differently than the usage message function. This function uses a POSIX syntax to define the function, whereas the usage message function uses Korn Shell Syntax. The reason for this is because there are no "local" variables in a POSIX function. So anything defined within a POSIX function becomes a global variable, which is what we want in a configuration function. We want this function to execute a configuration file and make those definitions available to the calling function, in this instance the basic template function "my_template_k93".

Since the Basic template function is defined as a Korn Shell function, it can and will have local variables. It will have values passed to it as command line options, local variables, global variables, and additional global variables dynamically defined from its configuration file.

Again, this configuration function contains embedded documentation identified as comments beginning with 4 #'s followed by a space. *From this point forward, this Embedded Documentation Indicator will be referenced in this book as EDI.*

The first executable line of the configuration function defines a shell variable named CFILE and assigns it a value pointing to a hidden file in the users' home directory. This file is named ".my_template01_k93.conf".

If this file exists and is a regular file, the file is executed as a "dot" script in the current shell environment. This means the script must have the correct shell code syntax or the calling script will exit with a syntax error. The script user may change the behavior of the shell function by modifying the parameters in the configuration file which may or may not exist under their own home directory. If the configuration file does not exist, then no configuration modifications are performed. The purpose of the dynamic configuration function is to provide the script user with additional capabilities for modifying the behavior of the shell function.

The script user now has multiple methods of controlling the behavior of the script function. They can specify command line options and/or they can define a configuration file under their own home directory. Normally the script user would only use command line options, but since the configuration file is executed as a "dot" script in the current shell environment, the user can include changes to modify any values they want. They can even include additional tasks to perform.

> *Understand this does not provide the user with any elevated permissions or authorizations, it only allows them to modify the behavior of a shell script they already have permission to execute.*

Another advanced shell script programming feature to recognize in the configuration function, is the use of the VERBOSE status messages.

```
(( VERBOSE == TRUE )) && print -- "# Configuration File: ${CFILE}"
...
...
...
(( VERBOSE == TRUE )) && cat ${CFILE}
```

It is recommended the advanced shell script programmer include copious status messages within their code so the script user may turn these messages "on" or "off" using the "-v" command line option. If the "-v" command line option is specified, the VERBOSE shell variable is assigned a value of TRUE. Then an arithmetic test is performed to determine if the value of the variable VERBOSE is equal to TRUE, if so the status message is printed. This technique is used throughout all examples in this book and leads us to the following *Shell Script Programming Guidelines* to be included in the Business Continuity plan:

- Every shell script function should include the "-v" command line option to toggle "on" the display of VERBOSE status messages.

- Every shell script function should include the "-V" command line option to toggle "on" the VERYVERB script debugging mode.

The next section of the script defines the main body of the shell script function named "my_template01_k93". Notice it is defined as a Korn Shell function, and since it is a Korn Shell function it can contain local variables.

```
function my_template01_k93 {
    typeset VERSION="1.0"
    typeset TRUE="0"
    typeset FALSE="1"
    typeset VERBOSE="${FALSE}"
    typeset VERYVERB="${FALSE}"
```

Local variables are defined in the Basic template using the "typeset" built-in command. It is important to know that any use of the typeset command within a Korn Shell function defines the variable a local variable. In this example several variables are defined and initialized. As a recommendation for Advanced Shell Script Programming Guidelines, the following shell variables should be defined and initialized in all shell script functions:

VERSION="X.X"

TRUE="0"

FALSE="1"

VERBOSE="${FALSE}"

VERYVERB="${FALSE}"

The initial values of the recommended variables may be different than shown above depending upon the needs and requirements of the shell script function being created.

The next section of code in the Basic template executes the configuration function previously discussed.

```
#### Set up a trap of the HUP signal to cause this script
#### to dynamically configure or reconfigure itself upon
#### receipt of the HUP signal.

    trap "configure_my_template01_k93 ${0}" HUP

#### Read the configuration file and initialize variables by
```

```
#### sending this script a HUP signal
kill -HUP ${$}
```

The execution of the configuration function is triggered by setting up a
signal "trap" and then sending the currently running template function the
trigger signal. In this instance the trigger is the HUP signal and it is sent to
the current PID using the "kill" command. When the current function
receives the HUP signal the trap is sprung and the configuration function
named "configure_my_template01_k93" is executed.

Again notice the embedded documentation using the EDI markup. These
comments will be extracted by the automated documentation generator.

The next section of code in the basic template processes the command
line options.

```
#### Process the command line options and arguments.
while getopts ":vv" OPTION
do
    case "${OPTION}" in
        'v') VERBOSE="${TRUE}";;
        'v') VERYVERB="${TRUE}";;
        '?') usagemsg_my_template01_k93 "${0}" && return 1 ;;
        ':') usagemsg_my_template01_k93 "${0}" && return 2 ;;
        '#') usagemsg_my_template01_k93 "${0}" && return 3 ;;
    esac
done

shift $(( ${OPTIND} - 1 ))
```

In this template only a couple of options are specified and processed by
the "getopts" built-in command. This is a standard built-in command in
multiple shells including Korn Shell, Bash, Z-shell, and others.

If errors are encountered during the command line option processing, the
usage message function is called, and the script returns to the calling script
or function.

If all command line options are processed successfully, the processed
command line arguments are "shifted" off the command line, and script
execution continues.

In this example the OPTIND variable is a local variable to the Korn Shell
function and does not need to be initialized at the beginning of the
function. However we will see that is not always true depending upon the

script interpreter and shell script function type. This will be addressed in a later chapter.

The next section of code in the Basic template performs error checking of the variables and values defined in the initialization section, configuration file, and command line option processing.

```
trap "usagemsg_my_template01_k93 ${0}" EXIT

#### Place any command line option error checking statements
#### here.  If an error is detected, print a message to
#### standard error, and return from this function with a
#### non-zero return code.  The "trap" statement will cause
#### the "usagemsg" to be displayed.

trap "-" EXIT
```

A trap is configured so that if a parameter value is incorrect, the usage message is automatically displayed before returning from the function. The error checking is performed by testing the parameter values to determine validity and if invalid, execute a "return" command. The "return" command springs the "EXIT" trap, displays the usage message, and returns to the calling script or function. This will also be discussed in greater detail in later chapters, it is enough for now to know these parameters should be tested and examined at this point in the script before proceeding any further.

Again notice the EDI markup comments.

The next section of the code is where the actual work of the function begins. At this point all the local variables have been defined, the configuration file has been processed, the command line options have been processed, and all parameters have been checked for errors or invalid values. The function is now ready to actually do something.

```
####
#### Your shell function should perform it's specific work here.
#### All work performed by your shell function should be coded
#### within this section of the function.  This does not mean that
#### your function should be called from here, it means the shell
#### code that performs the work of your function should be
#### incorporated into the body of this function.  This should
#### become your function.
####

(( VERBOSE  == TRUE )) && print -u 2 "# MSG Variable Value: ${MSG}"
print -- "${MSG}"
```

Again, more EDI markup documentation.

In this example, the Basic template simply displays the remaining command line arguments that were specified on the command line; not the options, just the arguments. The options were previously processed by the "getopts" function. A shell variable "MSG" is assigned all remaining command line arguments using "${@}", and the contents of the MSG variable are then displayed on standard output using the Korn shell "print" built-in command.

If the "-v" command line option was specified, then it was processed by the "getopts" function and set the value of the shell variable VERBOSE to TRUE. Therefore the arithmetic test will return TRUE and the status message will be displayed. The status message is displayed before displaying the command line arguments.

Finally in the last section of code in the basic template, the HUP signal trap is closed, and the function returns to the calling script or function.

```
trap "-" HUP
return 0
```

At this point all the functions, variables, files, and components are defined, however since everything is defined as a "function", nothing is executed until we call one of the functions. The last line of the basic template is a call to the function "my_template01_k93".

```
my_template01_k93 "${@}"
```

When executing the standalone script, all command line arguments are passed to the shell script function by specifying the "${@}" variable. This syntax causes variable substitution for all command line arguments to be placed on the command line, each command line argument in double quotes.

So the shell script function "my_template01_k93" is executed with all command line arguments from the command line when the standalone script was executed.

At this time, the reader will want to copy the source code from the Basic template in Appendix A to a file on your UNIX/Linux/Cygwin desktop for testing and reference.

If you choose to execute this Basic template shell script, you will need Korn Shell 93 installed at /usr/bin/ksh93 or you can change the SHEBANG line in the template to reference the location of the Korn Shell 93 interpreter on your system.

Now run some examples of executing the Basic template from the command line. It is assumed the standalone shell script containing the basic template has 755 (rwxr-xr-x) permissions:

```
$ ./my_template01_k93

$
```

Since the command shown above is executed with no command line arguments, nothing was displayed. Run it again with the "-?" command line argument to cause it to display the usage message:

```
$ ./my_template01_k93 -?

Program my_template01_k93

Place a brief description (< 255 chars ) of your shell
Function here.

Usage: my_template01_k93 [-?vV]

Where:
    -v = Verbose mode - displays my_template01_k93
         function info
    -V = Very Verbose Mode - debug output displayed
    -? = Help - display this message

Author: Your Name (YourEmailAddress @ domain.com )

"AutoContent" enabled

$
```

Next, run the script again with some command line arguments.

```
$ ./my_template01_k93 hello world
Hello world
$
```

Next, run the script including the "-v" command line option to turn on VERBOSE mode:

```
$ ./my_template01_k93 -v hello world
# Version...........: 1.0
# MSG Variable Value: hello world
Hello world
$
```

Next, run the script including the "-V" command line option to turn on X-Trace mode:

```
$ ./my_template01_k93 -V hello world
+ (( VERBOSE  == TRUE ))
+ MSG='hello world'
+ (( VERBOSE  == TRUE ))
+ print -- 'hello world'
hello world
+ trap â€" HUP
+ return 0
$
```

And finally, run the script with both "-v" and "-V" command line options:

```
$ ./my_template01_k93 -V -v hello world
+ (( VERBOSE  == TRUE ))
+ print -u 2 '# Version...........: 1.0'
# Version...........: 1.0
+ MSG='hello world'
+ (( VERBOSE  == TRUE ))
+ print -u 2 '# MSG Variable Value: hello world'
# MSG Variable Value: hello world
+ print -u 2 'hello world'
hello world
+ trap - HUP
+ return 0
$
```

In this examination of the Basic template we have discussed several concepts upon which we will expand in subsequent chapters. These concepts included:

- Reusable tasks written as functions

- Embedded documentation

- Usage message

- Dynamic configuration

- Command line option processing using "getopts"

- EDI markup for embedded comments

- Korn Shell vs POSIX functions

- Traps

- Variable typesets

- Local variables in functions

- Embedded status reporting

Chapter 3: The Intermediate Template

Next is a look at an intermediate level template which expands upon the concepts introduced in the previous chapter. As with the Basic template, the Intermediate template is used to illustrate how Business Continuity and Data Center Automation are the driving forces behind these Advanced Shell Script Programming techniques.

The Advanced Shell Script Programming technique added in this chapter is oriented around enabling "Multi-Shell" execution capabilities. This additional capability can be added to the Business Continuity Foundations table from the previous chapter as follows:

Business Continuity Foundations

- Shell Script Programming Policies
    - o Reusable tasks written as functions
    - o Embedded documentation
- Shell Scripting Guidelines
    - o **Multi-Shell Execution**
    - o Usage message
    - o Dynamic configuration
    - o Command line option processing using "getopts"
    - o Unique Variable Naming
- Shell Scripting Standards
    - o Grutatxt markup for embedded comments
- Shell Scripting Procedures
    - o ksh93 Function
    - o Traps
    - o Variable typesets
    - o Local variables in functions

o   Embedded status reporting

The goals and concepts remain the same, we are simply adding a new technique to expand the Advanced Programming style guide. The recommendations remain the same, the benefits remain the same, with some additions:

- Centralized location of code

- Repeatable and reusable code

- Standardized mechanisms for common tasks

- Code auditing and style guides

- Training

- Standardized Documentation

- Centralized and transferable knowledge base

- Cross-Platform portability

- Cross-Shell Portability

- Multi-Operating System Portability

The functions defined in the standalone Intermediate template script include the following:

- usagemsg_my_template02_zbksh

  o   Uses Korn Shell Style function definition

  o   Displays a usage message to standard output

- configure_my_template02_zbksh

  o   Uses POSIX style function definition

  o   Dynamic configuration of the template function

- my_template01_ksh93

  o   Uses Korn Shell style function definition

  o   Primary activities performed here

- Main body of the standalone script

  - Multi-Shell setup and configuration

The purpose of the Intermediate template is to illustrate Multi-shell execution capabilities, so the very first line of the script, the SHEBANG line, becomes highly significant and configurable:

```
#!/usr/bin/ksh93
#!/bin/bash
#!/bin/zsh
##################################################
####
#### This script will run in KornShell93, zshell, or Bash, all you need to do
#### is put the desired "shebang" line at the top of the script.
####
##################################################
```

The Intermediate template is now capable of being executed as a Korn Shell script, Bash Script, or in Z-Shell, and this capability is reflected in the stack of SHEBANG line choices at the top of the script. Understand the script interpreter must still be specified on the first line of the script, but it can be changed when porting the script between platforms, operating systems, architectures, or shells. In the multi-shell execution environment, the only modification to the shell script is to change the SHEBANG line to the appropriate script interpreter for the new environment. No other script changes are needed.

In the previous chapter, we stepped thru the Basic template from top to bottom. Because of the Multi-Shell capabilities, it is important to examine the main body of the shell script first before stepping thru the functions. In this standalone shell script, the main body of the script is at the bottom of the file and has the following content:

```
##################################################
####
#### Main Body of Script Begins Here
####
##################################################

TRUE="0"
FALSE="1"

####
#### Extract the "shebang" line from the beginning of the script

read SHEBANG < "${0}"
export SHEBANG

####
#### Test the "shebang" line to determine what shell interpreter is specified
```

```
        SHCODE="unknown"
        [[ "_${SHEBANG}" == _*/ksh*  ]] && SHCODE="korn"
        [[ "_${SHEBANG}" == _*/bash* ]] && SHCODE="bash"
        [[ "_${SHEBANG}" == _*/zsh*  ]] && SHCODE="zshell"
        export SHCODE

        ####
        #### Modify the commands and script according to the shell interpreter

        GBL_ECHO="echo -e"
        [[ "_${SHCODE}" == "_korn"   ]] && GBL_ECHO="print --"
        [[ "_${SHCODE}" == "_zshell" ]] && GBL_ECHO="print --" && emulate ksh93
        [[ "_${SHCODE}" == "_bash"   ]] && shopt -s extglob    # Turn on extended
globbing

        ####
        #### Call the script function to begin processing

        my_template02_zbksh "${@}"
```

In the Basic template, the main body of the script consisted of a single line which called the function named "my_template01_k93". In the main body of the Intermediate template, the multi-shell configuration activities are performed so the results are available as global variables to any and all functions that may be subsequently referenced.

The main body of the Intermediate script begins by initializing any global variables that may be needed by all components of the script. In this Intermediate script, these global variables consist of the following:

```
        TRUE="0"
        FALSE="1"
```

These variables define the values of TRUE and FALSE and will be used for a variety of purposes within each function.

The next step in the main body of the Intermediate template script, is to determine which shell script interpreter is designated on the SHEBANG line to execute the shell programming code. This can be done by reading the first line of the current script file and testing the obtained value against the file names of some known shell interpreters.

```
        ####
        #### Extract the "shebang" line from the beginning of the script

        read SHEBANG < "${0}"
        export SHEBANG

        ####
        #### Test the "shebang" line to determine what shell interpreter is
specified

        SHCODE="unknown"
        [[ "_${SHEBANG}" == _*/ksh*  ]] && SHCODE="korn"
        [[ "_${SHEBANG}" == _*/bash* ]] && SHCODE="bash"
        [[ "_${SHEBANG}" == _*/zsh*  ]] && SHCODE="zshell"
```

```
export SHCODE
```

In the Intermediate template, the value of the first line of the standalone shell script is tested to see if it specifies a Korn Shell interpreter by attempting to match the SHEBANG line value against a hardcoded value of "*/ksh*. If it matches, the SHCODE variable is initialized as "korn" and this variable will be used by subsequent commands to determine how to interpret the rest of the script. Similar tests and assignments are performed for "bash", and "Z-shell", as seen above.

At this point the Intermediate template has dynamically determined how it should interpret itself, selecting either Korn Shell, Bash, or Z-Shell. The template will use this information to configure itself accordingly. It will create a global shell variable whose value contains the appropriate output command for the designated shell interpreter.

```
####
#### Modify the commands and script according to the shell interpreter

GBL_ECHO="echo -e"
    [[ "_${SHCODE}" == "_korn"   ]] && GBL_ECHO="print --"
    [[ "_${SHCODE}" == "_zshell" ]] && GBL_ECHO="print --" && emulate ksh93
    [[ "_${SHCODE}" == "_bash"   ]] && shopt -s extglob    # Turn on extended
globbing
```

The default value of the GBL_ECHO variable will be initialized as "echo -e", which will work across most shells. Then it will begin testing the other shell interpreter possibilities. If the selected shell code interpreter is "korn" or "zshell", the GBL_ECHO variable will be initialized as "print --". Additionally if the shell interpreter is "zshell", the current shell environment will be configured to emulate Korn Shell.

If the shell interpreter is "bash", the extended globbing shell option is enabled to turn on numerous variable substitution capabilities similar to Korn Shell.

For the Intermediate template script, all the shell interpreter configurations are complete, so normal processing can now begin by calling one of the functions defined in the standalone script, specifically the function named "my_template02_zbksh":

```
####
#### Call the script function to begin processing

my_template02_zbksh "${@}"
```

Now go back to the top of the Intermediate template script and step thru the changes in each function. At the top of the script observe the usage message function which displays the instructions for executing the shell script. It provides a description of the function, lists command line options, syntax, and any other information the function programmer thinks is relevant to the shell script programmer. You will see some differences between the Basic and Intermediate versions.

Basic Template Version:

```
function usagemsg_my_template01_k93 {
   print "
Program: my_template01_k93

Place a brief description ( < 255 chars ) of your shell
function here.

Usage: ${1##*/} [-?vv]

   where:
      -v = Verbose mode - displays my_template01_k93 function info
      -V = Very Verbose Mode - debug output displayed
      -? = Help - display this message

Author: Your Name (YourEmail@address.com)
\"AutoContent\" enabled
"
}
```

Intermediate Template Version:

```
function usagemsg_my_template02_zbksh {
   CMD_ECHO="${GBL_ECHO:-echo -e }"
   ${CMD_ECHO} ""
   ${CMD_ECHO} "${1:+Program: ${1}}${2:+          Version: ${2}}"

   ${CMD_ECHO} "
Place a brief description ( < 255 chars ) of your shell
function here.

Usage: ${1##*/} [-?vv] [-u] [-l]

   where:
      -u = Convert command line arguments to upper case
      -l = Convert command line arguments to lower case
      -v = Verbose mode - displays my_template02_zbksh function info
      -V = Very Verbose Mode - debug output displayed
      -? = Help - display this message

Author: Your Name (YourEmail@address.com)

\"AutoContent\" enabled
\"Multi-Shell\" enabled
"
}
```

In the intermediate version, several new variables are introduced, these include:

- ${GBL_ECHO}
- ${CMD_ECHO}
- ${1}
- ${2}

One of the major differences between shells, is the mechanism to display output. In Korn Shell "echo", "print", and "printf" can be used. In Bash "echo" and "printf" are standard built-in shell commands, but not "print". Whereas Z-shell can be configured to behave like Korn Shell and support all three output commands. In order to accommodate the widest range of shell interpreters, the output command should be *variablized* so that it may be dynamically configured for any shell interpreter.

In the usagemsg function, it can be seen that a variable called CMD_ECHO is initialized using the value of GBL_ECHO as follows:

```
CMD_ECHO="${GBL_ECHO:-echo -e }"
```

The shell variable GBL_ECHO is a global variable initialized in the main body of the script. The variable substitution operator ":-" is used to dynamically assign a value to the shell variable CMD_ECHO as follows:

> If the value of GBL_ECHO is unset or null, "echo -e" is assigned to the value of CMD_ECHO.

> Otherwise the value of GBL_ECHO is assigned to the value of CMD_ECHO

The next obvious difference between the Basic and Intermediate usagemsg functions, is the hard-coded "print" command has been substituted with the variable:

> ${CMD_ECHO}

This enables the usage message to be displayed regardless of which shell is executing the function. This is because the value of CMD_ECHO will dynamically contain the appropriate built-in command associated with the shell interpreter currently executing the shell environment.

Also observe the Intermediate template version of this function includes a couple of additional functions:

```
-u = Convert command line arguments to upper case
-l = Convert command line arguments to lower case
```

These options are included in the intermediate template for the purpose of demonstrating error checking of command line options, which will be discussed a little later in the chapter.

The standard command line options are included:

- -v: Display verbose status messages as specified by the function programmer

- -V: Display very verbose messaging, which turns on the X-Trace mode shell option. This is equivalent of running the "set -x" command. If you are unfamiliar with X-Trace mode, you will want to look this up on a Basic shell programming manual.

The next section of interest from the Intermediate template is the same as in the Basic template, which is the documentation area:

```
####################################################
####
#### Description:
####
#### Place a full text description of your shell function here.
####
#### Assumptions:
####
#### Provide a list of assumptions your shell function makes,
#### with a description of each assumption.
####
#### Dependencies:
####
#### Provide a list of dependencies your shell function has,
#### with a description of each dependency.
####
#### Products:
####
#### Provide a list of output your shell function produces,
#### with a description of each product.
####
#### Configured Usage:
####
#### Describe how your shell function should be used.
####
#### Details:
####
#### Place nothing here, the details are your shell function.
####
####################################################
```

We will dispense with providing a detailed description of this section again.

Next is an examination of the differences between the configuration POSIX functions in the Basic and Intermediate templates.

Basic Template Configuration Function:

```
configure_my_template01_k93()
{
####
#### Notice this function is a POSIX function so that it can see local
#### and global variables from calling functions and scripts.
####
#### Configuration parameters can be stored in a file and
#### this script can be dynamically reconfigured by sending
#### the running script a HUP signal using the kill command.
####
#### Configuration variables can be defined in the configuration file using
#### the same syntax as defining a shell variable, e.g.: VARIABLE="value"

    CFILE=~/.my_template01_k93.conf

    (( VERBOSE == TRUE )) && print -- "# Configuration File: ${CFILE}"

    if [[ -f ${CFILE} ]]
    then
        (( VERBOSE == TRUE )) && cat ${CFILE}
        . ${CFILE}
    fi

    return 0
}
```

Intermediate Template Configuration Function:

```
configure_my_template02_zbksh()
{
####
#### Notice this function is a POSIX function so that it can see local
#### and global variables from calling functions and scripts.
####
#### Configuration parameters can be stored in a file and
#### this script can be dynamically reconfigured by sending
#### the running script a HUP signal using the kill command.
####
#### Configuration variables can be defined in the configuration file using
#### the same syntax as defining a shell variable, e.g.: VARIABLE="value"

    CMD_ECHO="${GBL_ECHO:-echo -e }"

    [[ "_${1}" != "_" ]] && MYT_CFILE=~/.${1}.conf

    (( VERBOSE == TRUE )) && ${CMD_ECHO} "# Configuration File: ${MYT_CFILE}"

    if [[ -f ${MYT_CFILE} ]]
    then
        (( VERBOSE == TRUE )) && cat ${MYT_CFILE}
        . ${MYT_CFILE}
    fi

    return 0
}
```

The variable CMD_ECHO is again initialized inside the Intermediate template configuration function using the value of GBL_ECHO. And in this version, the configuration file name is assembled from the value of the first command line parameter followed by the suffix ".conf". Before using the value of the first command line parameter, it is tested to verify it contains a non-null value. Also the first command line parameter is tested to verify the value corresponds to a file that exists, and it is a regular file.

The purpose of the configuration function in the Intermediate template is the same as in the Basic template, which is to provide a dynamic mechanism of configuring the shell script function. It executes a configuration file which is assumed to contain shell code. Usually this file contains shell variable definitions, however it may contain any shell code desired, including references to outside functions, applications, or utilities.

Again, this Intermediate template configuration function contains embedded documentation identified as comments beginning with 4 #'s followed by a space (####).

The next section of the Intermediate template script contains the commands which comprise the primary purpose of the script. This is a function named "my_template02_zbksh" and is defined using the Korn Shell style definition syntax. One of the features of using this syntax is the shell script programmer will have the ability to assign local variables inside the function. However if this same script is executed as a Bash script, all variables become global variables regardless of the function definition syntax or use of the "typeset" built-in command.

> NOTE: In Korn Shell 93, if a variable is initialized inside a
> Korn Shell style function using the 'typeset" built-in
> command, the variable becomes a local variable to the
> function.

It is normally best practice to initialize all local variables at the beginning of each function, however some shell interpreters do not support local variable definitions. To accommodate these shell interpreters, it is best practice to use variable names that are unique to each function for local variables. This can be observed in the variable initialization of the "my_template02_zbksh" function:

```
typeset TRUE="${TRUE:-0}"
typeset FALSE="${FALSE:-1}"
typeset VERBOSE="${VERBOSE:-${FALSE}}"
```

```
typeset VERYVERB="${VERYVERB:-${FALSE}}"
typeset OPTIND="1"
typeset CMD_ECHO="${GBL_ECHO:-echo -e }"
typeset MYT_PROGRAM="my_template02_zbksh"
typeset MYT_VERSION="1.0"
typeset MYT_TGGLEUP="${FALSE}"
typeset MYT_TGGLELO="${FALSE}"
typeset MYT_ARGVALU=""
```

The global variables have common names that are used in every script where the variable is needed. The local variables in this instance all begin with the prefix "MYT_". The variable prefix should be unique and different to each function. This practice will reduce the possibility of errors when executing this script between multiple shells where local variables may not be supported.

Notice the variable definition of OPTIND.

OPTIND is a variable used with the "getopts" function to reference the last command line option processed. An anomaly of a shell interpreter that does not support local variables, such as Bash, is that if a function is called from a function while processing command line options, then the value of the OPTIND variable will be corrupted in the called function. To avoid this issue, it is recommended that the OPTIND variable be initialized at the beginning of any function using the "getopts" function.

The next section of code in the intermediate template executes the configuration function. Here it is called directly as a function instead of using the "trap" and "kill" commands. Either method can be used. The difference is that when using the "trap" and "kill" commands, the function can be dynamically reconfigured at any time by trapping an internal or external HUP signal. If the configuration function is called directly, then it is not dynamic and will not be re-called if a HUP signal is sent to the function. In fact, if the HUP signal is not trapped, the script will be terminated by the HUP signal.

```
configure_my_template02_zbksh "${MYT_PROGRAM}"
```

Notice the first command line parameter is the local variable MYT_PROGRAM which contains the name of the intermediate template function.

The command line option processing section of the intermediate template is very similar to this same section of code in the basic template. The logic is the same with a couple of additional options. These new options allow the user to flip toggle switches from FALSE to TRUE. Specifically, it allows the script user to flip a switch to convert the command line parameters to all uppercase or all lower case characters. This capability will be demonstrated when the script is executed.

```
#### Process the command line options and arguments.

while getopts ":vVul" OPTION
do
   case "${OPTION}" in
      'u') MYT_TGGLEUP="${TRUE}";;
      'l') MYT_TGGLELO="${TRUE}";;
      'v') VERBOSE="${TRUE}";;
      'V') VERYVERB="${TRUE}";;
      '?') usagemsg_my_template02_zbksh "${MYT_PROGRAM}" "${MYT_VERSION}"
&& return 1 ;;
      ':') usagemsg_my_template02_zbksh "${MYT_PROGRAM}" "${MYT_VERSION}"
&& return 2 ;;
      '#') usagemsg_my_template02_zbksh "${MYT_PROGRAM}" "${MYT_VERSION}"
&& return 3 ;;
   esac
done

shift $(( ${OPTIND} - 1 ))
```

Additionally, the command line arguments, when calling the "usagemsg_my_template02_zbksh" function, have been changed from the Basic template. In the Intermediate template, local variables are used to identify the program name and version number. The use of these variables can be observed in the "getopts" code snippet above.

Other than these differences, the "getopts" command line processing is the same as previously examined.

In the Basic template discussion, the error checking section was mentioned, but skipped because there were not really any variable values that required checking. In the Intermediate template, we have introduced a couple of command line options and values that may conflict with each other. For example, if the user specifies both options (-u and –l) on the command line, this would be considered a conflict. The user would be instructing the script to convert the command line parameters to upper case and lower case simultaneously. This does not make sense programmatically, so logic is added to the script to check for this condition. If it exists, display an error and the script usage message, then exit the script.

```
####################################################

#### Place any command line option error checking statements
#### here.  If an error is detected, print a message to
```

```
#### standard error, and return from this function with a
#### non-zero return code.  The "trap" statement will cause
#### the "usagemsg" to be displayed.

    trap "usagemsg_my_template02_zbksh ${MYT_PROGRAM} ${MYT_VERSION}" EXIT

    if (( MYT_TGGLEUP == TRUE )) &&
       (( MYT_TGGLELO == TRUE ))
    then
        ${CMD_ECHO} "# ERROR: Do not specify both upper and lower case
conversion together"
        return 11
    fi

    trap "-" EXIT
```

In the above code snippet, observe the "if" statement that checks to see if
the value of the local variables named "MYT_TGGLEUP" and
"MYT_TGGLELO" are both equal to TRUE. If both values are TRUE,
an error message is displayed, and the script returns to the calling function
or script with a return code of "11".

Also observe this "return" is occurring within an "EXIT" trap, which will
also cause the specified command to be executed. In this instance the
specified command is the function named
"usagemsg_my_template02_zbksh".

Again notice the EDI markup comments.

Once all variables have been initialized, configuration values have been
read, command line options have been processed, and no potential
conflicts or invalid values exist, then it is safe to proceed with the function
activities. It is usually a good idea at this point in the function to allow the
script user to display the configuration information that will be used
during the execution of the function. This can be specified on the
command line using the "-v" option to turn on VERBOSE mode, or with
the "-V" option to turn on VERYVERB X-Trace mode.

In the Intermediate template, observe that if VERBOSE mode is turned
on, it will display the VERSION number and the remaining command
line parameters.

```
##################################################

    (( VERYVERB == TRUE )) && set -x
    (( VERBOSE  == TRUE )) && ${CMD_ECHO} "# Program Name......:
${MYT_PROGRAM}"
    (( VERBOSE  == TRUE )) && ${CMD_ECHO} "# Version..........:
${MYT_VERSION}"

    for MYT_ARGVALU in "${@}"
    do
```

```
        (( VERBOSE  == TRUE )) && ${CMD_ECHO} "# Command Line Arg..:
${MYT_ARGVALU}"
     done

  ##################################################
```

As much or as little information can be displayed as desired, it is up to the function programmer to determine what information would be valuable to the script programmer and user if they specified the VERBOSE mode option on the command line.

Notice in the code snippet above, all the remaining command line parameters are displayed using a "for" loop. The VERBOSE value test performed using arithmetic test syntax, is inside the loop so it will be performed for each command line parameter. This test could be performed outside the loop as well, that code would look like this:

```
  ##################################################

     (( VERYVERB == TRUE )) && set -x
     (( VERBOSE  == TRUE )) && ${CMD_ECHO} "# Program Name......:
${MYT_PROGRAM}"
     (( VERBOSE  == TRUE )) && ${CMD_ECHO} "# Version..........:
${MYT_VERSION}"

     if (( VERBOSE  == TRUE ))
     then
       for MYT_ARGVALU in "${@}"
       do
         ${CMD_ECHO} "# Command Line Arg..: ${MYT_ARGVALU}"
       done
     fi

  ##################################################
```

The second method is more efficient code, however the first method is easier to read. Either method is correct syntactically, it is up to the script programmer to decide which method they prefer to use.

> ***Programming TIP:*** Variables inside an arithmetic statement do not require the "$" at the beginning of the variable name, as you can see in the above code snippets. The variable VERBOSE does not have the "$" at the beginning because it is used inside an arithmetic statement. This syntax is true for ANY arithmetic statement such as an arithmetic "if" statement, array indexes, variable indexes, etc.

As with the Basic template, the only action performed by this function is to display the command line parameters. However this time the Intermediate function allows the script programmer or user to specify a couple of new command line options; Convert to upper case; Convert to lower case; or do no conversion at all.

```
####################################################

####
#### Your shell function should perform its specific work here.
#### All work performed by your shell function should be coded
#### within this section of the function.  This does not mean that
#### your function should be called from here, it means the shell
#### code that performs the work of your function should be
#### incorporated into the body of this function.  This should
#### become your function.
####

   if (( ${#@} > 0 ))
   then
       MYT_MSG="${@}"
   fi

   if [[ "_${MYT_MSG}" != "_" ]]
   then
       (( MYT_TGGLEUP == TRUE )) && typeset -u MYT_MSG="${MYT_MSG}"
       (( MYT_TGGLELO == TRUE )) && typeset -l MYT_MSG="${MYT_MSG}"

       (( VERBOSE   == TRUE )) && ${CMD_ECHO} "# MYT_MSG Variable Value:
${MYT_MSG}"
       ${CMD_ECHO} "${MYT_MSG}"
   fi
```

The first "if" statement above performs an arithmetic test on the number of command line parameters to determine if this value is greater than zero (0). If so, it assigns all remaining command line arguments to the local variable "MYT_MSG".

> **Programming TIP:** The default character used to separate each command line parameter when it is assigned to the "MYT_MSG" variable can be changed using the **IFS** environment variable. For example if you wanted a colon (:) delimiter between each parameter, you could change the IFS variable. That code would look like this:
>
> ```
> IFS=":"
> MYT_MSG="${*}"
> IFS=$' \t\n'
> ```

The next statement in the Intermediate template tests the value of the variable "MYT_MSG" to see if it is non-null. It performs this test because the script user may or may not have entered any parameters on the command line.

Also remember the configuration file: a value could have been assigned to the variable "MYT_MSG" inside the configuration file. So even if the script user did not enter any command line parameters, the value of "MYT_MSG" may be non-null because it was assigned a value in the configuration file.

Assuming the variable "MYT_MSG" has a non-null value, it will pass the "if" statement test and then perform the upper or lower case conversions, if specified by the script programmer or user.

```
(( MYT_TGGLEUP == TRUE )) && typeset -u MYT_MSG="${MYT_MSG}"
(( MYT_TGGLELO == TRUE )) && typeset -l MYT_MSG="${MYT_MSG}"
```

The "typeset" built-in command is used to perform the case conversion to upper or lower case. This is a valid command in Korn Shell, Bash, and Z-shell. If you wish to perform similar conversions in other shells, you may need to test which shell interpreter is being used (${SHCODE}) and use the "tr" command to perform the conversion in those other shells.

At this point in the Intermediate template, it displays the value of the variable "MYT_MSG" using the appropriate command in the current shell interpreter. The command is contained in the value of the "CMD_ECHO" variable.

Programming TIP: In the Intermediate template a code snippet is shown describing "while" loop processing.

```
#### Example Syntax:
####    grep X file > /tmp/tmp${$}.out
####    IDX="0"
####    while read VALUE
####    do ARRY[IDX++]="${VALUE}"
####    done < /tmp/tmp${$}.out
####    rm -f /tmp/tmp${$}.out
####    for i in "${ARRY[@]}"; do echo ${i}; done
####
```

Even though the Intermediate template does not use a "while" loop, it is worthwhile to discuss this syntax at this time. This logic is oriented around the differences between the shells when defining variables inside a "while" or "until" loop.

In Korn shell, the following would be valid syntax:

```
IDX="0"
grep X somefile | while read VALUE
do
    ARRY[IDX++]="${VALUE}"
done

for i in "${ARRY[@]}"
```

```
do
    print "${i}"
done
```

It is valid syntax in Bash as well, however the result is different. The pipe
(|) symbol causes both Korn and Bash to invoke a subshell when sending
the output from the grep command into the while loop. The difference
occurs when the "while" loop ends. In Korn shell, any variables defined
or assigned in the subshell are visible in the parent shell, in Bash they are
not. So in Bash, any assignments to the "ARRY" variable are lost when
the "while" loop ends. The "for" loop would not display anything because
the ARRY variable contains no values.

To fix this difference in behavior, use the following syntax, yes it is
inefficient, and yes it is ugly, but it works:

```
grep X file > /tmp/tmp${$}.out

IDX="0"
while read VALUE
do
    ARRY[IDX++]="${VALUE}"
done < /tmp/tmp${$}.out

rm -f /tmp/tmp${$}.out

for i in "${ARRY[@]}"
do
    echo "${i}"
done
```

The last statement of the function "my_template02_zbksh" is to return
with a zero (0) or TRUE return code to the calling function or script. In
this instance it would return to the main body of the script and since it
was the last statement of the script, it would then exit to the calling shell.

> ***Programming TIP:*** The exit code of any script is derived from
> the exit or return code of the last command executed. So if the
> last command executed was a function, and the calling script
> does not have an exit statement, the exit code of the main script
> will be the exit code of the function.

At this time, the reader will want to copy the content of the Intermediate
template from Appendix B to a file on your desktop for testing and
reference. If you choose to execute this Intermediate template shell script,
you will want to use a variety of shell interpreters to see that it works
across multiple shells. In this case you may want to install Korn Shell 93,

Bash, Zsh. You can also run these scripts in a Cygwin Bash shell in Windows.

> **NOTE: Remember to change the SHEBANG line in the template to reference the location of the shell interpreter you want to use each time you run the script.**

Now execute some examples using the Intermediate template from the command line. It is assumed the standalone shell script containing the basic template has 755 (rwxr-xr-x) permissions.

In this first script execution, run the script as a "ksh93" script. Edit the script and specify the full path file name of the Korn Shell 93 interpreter as the SHEBANG line:

```
#!/usr/bin/ksh93
#!/bin/bash
#!/bin/zsh
#################################################
####
#### This script will run in KornShell93, Zshell, or Bash, all you need to
do
#### is put the desired "shebang" line at the top of the script.
####
#################################################
```

Then run the script:

```
$ ./my_template02_zbksh
$
```

Since there were no command line arguments, nothing was displayed. Run it again with the "-?" command line argument to cause it to display the usage message:

```
$ ./.my_template02_zbksh -?

Program: my_template02_zbksh          Version: 1.0

Place a brief description ( < 255 chars ) of your shell
function here.

Usage: my_template02_zbksh [-?vV] [-u] [-l]

    Where:
       -u = Convert command line arguments to upper case
       -l = Convert command line arguments to lower case
       -v = Verbose mode - displays my_template02_zbksh function info
       -V = Very Verbose Mode - debug output displayed
       -? = Help - display this message

Author: Your Name (YourEmail@address.com)

"AutoContent" enabled
"Multi-Shell" enabled
```

Now edit the configuration file and assign a default value to the variable "MYT_MSG".

```
vi ~/my_template02_zbksh.conf
MYT_MSG="Hello World!"
:wq
```

Then run the script again with no command line arguments:

```
$ ./my_template02.zbksh
Hello World!
$
```

Now run the script using the upper case conversion option, then the lower case conversion option, then both options at the same time.

```
$ ./my_template02.zbksh -u
HELLO WORLD!

$ ./my_template02.zbksh -l
hello world!

$ ./my_template02.zbksh -u -l
# ERROR: Do not specify both upper and lower case conversion together

Program: my_template02_zbksh          Version: 1.0

Place a brief description ( < 255 chars ) of your shell
function here.

Usage: my_template02_zbksh [-?vV] [-u] [-l]

    Where:
      -u = Convert command line arguments to upper case
      -l = Convert command line arguments to lower case
      -v = Verbose mode - displays my_template02_zbksh function info
      -V = Very Verbose Mode - debug output displayed
      -? = Help - display this message

Author: Your Name (YourEmail@address.com)

"AutoContent" enabled
"Multi-Shell" enabled
```

Now change the SHEBANG line to bash, and re-run the script commands. The results should be the same.

```
vi my_template02_zbksh
#!/bin/bash
#!/usr/bin/ksh93
#!/bin/zsh
##################################################
####
#### This script will run in KornShell93, Zshell, or Bash, all you need to do
#### is put the desired "shebang" line at the top of the script.
####
##################################################
...
```

```
...
...
:wq

$ ./my_template02.zbksh -u
HELLO WORLD!

$ ./my_template02.zbksh -l
hello world!

$ ./my_template02.zbksh -u -l
# ERROR: Do not specify both upper and lower case conversion together

Program: my_template02_zbksh          Version: 1.0

Place a brief description ( < 255 chars ) of your shell
function here.

Usage: my_template02_zbksh [-?vV] [-u] [-l]

    Where:
      -u = Convert command line arguments to upper case
      -l = Convert command line arguments to lower case
      -v = Verbose mode - displays my_template02_zbksh function info
      -V = Very Verbose Mode - debug output displayed
      -? = Help - display this message

Author: Your Name (YourEmail@address.com)

"AutoContent" enabled
"Multi-Shell" enabled
```

Re-run the script as many times as you want, changing the SHEBANG
line for each new shell interpreter you want to test. Use the "-v" and "-V"
options to display the VERBOSE and VERYVERB output.

In this examination of the Intermediate template, it is seen that shell
scripts can dynamically configure themselves to execute commands
appropriate to the current shell interpreter.

It is also shown that a shell script template structure that can be modified
and reused for any shell script.

What you have seen so far is in the context of standalone scripts. In the
next chapter we will introduce the concept of shell function libraries and
how to use these libraries across multiple shell interpreters, even those
that do not support function libraries.

Chapter 4: The Library Template

In this chapter we will externalize the components of the standalone shell scripts into function libraries. This will provide centralized locations where function programmers can make their code available for use by other function and script programmers. Projects can be broken up into individual tasks and the results deposited into libraries for all to use and expand upon. And along this line of thought, the Intermediate template will be expanded and used to create a Library Function template. This new function will begin where we left off in the previous chapter and expand our programming capabilities into the utilization of shell scripts existing in a function library.

So in addition to the changes required to the template script, we will also examine the concept of "function library" and how to create/use these entities.

Also included is a discussion of how the use of function libraries are important in Business Continuity and Data Center Automation.

The Advanced Shell Script Programming technique being added in this chapter will be referred to as "Function Libraries" and it will be added to the table of Business Continuity Foundations:

Business Continuity Foundations

- Shell Script Programming Policies
    - o Reusable tasks written as functions
    - o Embedded documentation
    - o *Function Libraries*
- Shell Scripting Guidelines
    - o Multi-Shell Execution
    - o Usage message
    - o Dynamic configuration
    - o Command line option processing using "getopts"

- o   Unique Variable Naming
- Shell Scripting Standards
    - o   Grutatxt markup for embedded comments
- Shell Scripting Procedures
    - o   ksh93 Function
    - o   Traps
    - o   Variable typesets
    - o   Local variables in functions
    - o   Embedded status reporting

The functions defined in the Library Function template script include the following:

- usagemsg_my_template03_zbksh
    - o   Uses Korn Shell Style function definition
    - o   Displays a usage message to standard output
- configure_my_template03_zbksh
    - o   Uses POSIX style function definition
    - o   Dynamic configuration of the template function
- my_template03_zbksh
    - o   Uses Korn Shell style function definition
    - o   Primary activities performed here
- Main body of the standalone script
    - o   Multi-Shell setup and configuration
    - o   Function Libraries setup and configuration

The purpose of the Library Function template is to introduce the concept of shell script function libraries. We will still be using a standalone script to illustrate this capability and much of the code will be similar to the

Intermediate template. However there will be significant changes to the main body of the script and the way I/O is handled. The primary purpose of this chapter is to provide a detailed description of how to create and utilize a shell script function library.

As in the Intermediate template, the Library template will also be Multi-shell Enabled. This means it will be executable by multiple shell interpreters, so the shell script programmer may specify a different SHEBANG line depending upon how they want the script to be executed. The selected script interpreter will be identified by the first line of the standalone shell script.

```
#!/usr/bin/ksh93
#!/bin/bash
#!/bin/zsh
#################################################
####
#### This script will run in KornShell93, Zshell, or Bash, all you need to
do
#### is put the desired "shebang" line at the top of the script.
####
#################################################
```

The Library template will be executable as a Korn Shell script, Bash Script, or in Z-Shell, and this capability is reflected in the stack of SHEBANG line choices at the top of the script. Again, the script interpreter must still be specified on the first line of the script, but it can be changed when porting the script between platforms, operating systems, architectures, or shells. In the Shell Script Function Library execution environment, it may be necessary to modify the SHEBANG line and the location of the function libraries, depending upon where they may exist when porting a shell script to a new environment.

As in the discussion of the Intermediate template, we started at the bottom of the standalone shell script, we will do the same in this Library template discussion. Shown below is the shell script code for the main body of the Library template standalone shell script:

```
#################################################
####
#### Main Body of Script Begins Here
####
#################################################

####
#### Identify the function library directories to search
#### in the FPATH environment variable

FPATH=~/functions/adv_zbksh:~/functions:/usr/local/functions
export FPATH
```

```
####
#### Define the values for TRUE and FALSE,
#### In shell think, TRUE is zero (0) and FALSE is non-zero.

TRUE="0"
FALSE="1"

####
#### Extract the "shebang" line from the beginning of the script

read SHEBANG < "${0}"
export SHEBANG

####
#### Test the "shebang" line to determine what shell interpreter is
specified
SHCODE="unknown"
[[ "_${SHEBANG}" == _*/ksh*  ]] && SHCODE="korn"
[[ "_${SHEBANG}" == _*/bash* ]] && SHCODE="bash"
[[ "_${SHEBANG}" == _*/zsh*  ]] && SHCODE="zshell"
export SHCODE

####
#### Modify the shell specific commands and script according to the shell
interpreter
GBL_ECHO="echo -e"
[[ "_${SHCODE}" == "_korn"   ]] && GBL_ECHO="print --"
[[ "_${SHCODE}" == "_zshell" ]] && GBL_ECHO="print --" && emulate ksh93
[[ "_${SHCODE}" == "_bash"   ]] && shopt -s extglob    # Turn on extended
globbing

####
#### For those shell interpreters that do not directly support function
libraries,
#### cache all the *_zbksh functions found in the FPATH directories.
####

if [[ "_${SHCODE}" == "_zshell" ]] ||
   [[ "_${SHCODE}" == "_bash"   ]]
then

#### Loop thru each directory in the FPATH list using a colon (:)
delimeter.
#### Process each directory in reverse order to simulate results of
#### searching the FPATH directory.

    IFS=":"
    FDIRS=( ${FPATH} )
    IFS=$' \t\n'

    END=${#FDIRS[@]}
    for (( IDX=END-1; IDX>=0; --IDX ))
    do
        FDIR="${FDIRS[${IDX}]}"

#### Gather a list of functions ending in *_zbksh from the directory and
loop
#### thru each file using a “for” loop.

        for FUNC in ${FDIR}/*_zbksh
        do
####
#### Check each *_zbksh file to see if it starts with a function, if so
#### cache it in the current environment by running it as as a "dot"
script.
####
            if head -1 "${FUNC}" 2>/dev/null | egrep 'function|\(\)' >
/dev/null 2>&1
                then
                    . "${FUNC}"
```

```
              fi
          done
      done

      IFS=$' \t\n'

  fi


  ####
  #### Call the script function to begin processing
  my_template03_zbksh "${@}"
```

The first executable statement in the main body of the shell script defines an environment variable named FPATH. This variable defines a list of directories containing shell script functions that may be searched when an undefined function is called. The directories in the FPATH variable are searched in the order in which they appear in the list and if the function is found, it is sourced and executed. The colon (:) character is used as the delimiter between each directory. The FPATH variable is similar in form and function to the PATH variable, which exists in most shells. The FPATH variable is a built-in feature of Korn Shell, but is not a standard part of Bash or recognized by Z-shell.

In the Multi-Shell environment described here, we will use the FPATH variable as designed when the script code is being processed by a Korn Shell script interpreter. When processed by other script interpreters, some additional commands will be needed to search the FPATH directories for functions. In fact the only differences in the main body part between the Intermediate and Libraries templates, are the definition of the FPATH variable and the commands to process the directories defined in the FPATH variable by selected shells.

Since we have already discussed the definition of the FPATH variable, and we have already discussed the other parts of the script in the previous chapter, we will skip to the commands used to process the contents of the FPATH variable. These commands are only executed if the shell script interpreter is NOT Korn Shell as shown in the following code:

```
  if [[ "_${SHCODE}" == "_zshell" ]] ||
     [[ "_${SHCODE}" == "_bash" ]]
  then

  #### Loop thru each directory in the FPATH list using a colon (:)
delimeter.
  #### Process each directory in reverse order to simulate results of
  #### searching the FPATH directory.

      IFS=":"
      FDIRS=( ${FPATH} )
```

```
        IFS=$' \t\n'

        END=${#FDIRS[@]}
        for (( IDX=END-1; IDX>=0; --IDX ))
        do
            FDIR="${FDIRS[${IDX}]}"

    #### Gather a list of functions ending in *_zbksh from the directory and
loop
    #### thru each file using a "for" loop.

            for FUNC in ${FDIR}/*_zbksh
            do
    ####
    #### Check each *_zbksh file to see if it starts with a function, if so
    #### cache it in the current environment by running it as as a "dot"
script.
    ####
                if head -1 "${FUNC}" 2>/dev/null | egrep 'function|\(\)' >
/dev/null 2>&1
                then
                    . "${FUNC}"
                fi
            done
        done

        IFS=$' \t\n'

    fi
```

The above snippet of code will search all the directories listed in the FPATH variable for filenames ending in "_zbksh". It will then search each file that it finds to determine if the file contains a Korn shell or POSIX function. If so, it will source and cache each function in the current shell environment.

Notice the directories defined in the FPATH variable are processed in the reverse order in which they are defined. This is because the normal Korn Shell processing of the FPATH variable will search the directories in the defined order. The *first* matching function it finds will cause the search to stop and the function will be sourced, cached, and executed.

The above FPATH code sources and caches **ALL** functions it finds. Therefore if a matching function appears in more than one directory in the FPATH list, the last one sourced and cached will be the one used and executed if called. So in order to emulate the normal Korn Shell processing of the FPATH variable, it needs to search the directories of the FPATH variable in reverse order. This is why the arithmetic "for" loop processes the directories in reverse order, so the resulting cached functions is the last instance processed, which matches the "first found" behavior when processed in Korn Shell.

The order of processing of the files in each directory is irrelevant because each function should be defined in a separate file with a file name that matches the function name. Therefore there can only be one file in each directory with each unique function name.

> **NOTE: It is important to recognize the multi-shell processing of the FPATH directories assumes that all functions are individually defined in filenames ending with "_zbksh".**

The function declaration must be the first line of each file and may be a Korn Shell or POSIX style definition.

The following code extracts the first line of the discovered function file and tests it to determine if it contains the string "function" or the string "()". If so, the function is sourced, and cached as a "dot" script.

```
####
#### Check each *_zbksh file to see if it starts with a function, if so
#### cache it in the current environment by running it as as a "dot"
script.
####
        if head -1 "${FUNC}" 2>/dev/null | egrep 'function|\(\)' > /dev/null
2>&1
        then
              . "${FUNC}"
        fi
```

After this long discussion of the FPATH variable, and the how, what, and why of its processing, we are ready to move on and see the other differences between the Intermediate and Library templates.

The last line of the main body of the standalone script is a call to the function "my_template03_zbksh".

```
####
#### Call the script function to begin processing
my_template03_zbksh "${@}"
```

Now go back to the top of the Library template script and step thru the changes in each function. At the top of the script you will again see the usage message function which displays the instructions for executing the shell script. It provides a description of the function, lists command line options, syntax, and any other information the function programmer thinks is relevant to the script programmer or user. You will see some differences between the Intermediate and Library versions.

Intermediate Template Version:

```
function usagemsg_my_template02_zbksh {
    CMD_ECHO="${GBL_ECHO:-echo -e }"
    ${CMD_ECHO} ""
    ${CMD_ECHO} "${1:+Program: ${1}}${2:+          Version: ${2}}"

    ${CMD_ECHO} "
Place a brief description ( < 255 chars ) of your shell
function here.

Usage: ${1##*/} [-?vV] [-u] [-l]

    Where:
      -u = Convert command line arguments to upper case
      -l = Convert command line arguments to lower case
      -v = Verbose mode - displays my_template02_zbksh function info
      -V = Very Verbose Mode - debug output displayed
      -? = Help - display this message

Author: Your Name (YourEmail@address.com)

\"AutoContent\" enabled
\"Multi-Shell\" enabled
"
}
```

Library Template Version:

```
function usagemsg_my_template03_zbksh {
    stderr_zbksh ""
    stderr_zbksh "${1:+Program: ${1}}${2:+          Version: ${2}}"
    stderr_zbksh ""
    stderr_zbksh "Place a brief description ( < 255 chars ) of your shell"
    stderr_zbksh "function here."
    stderr_zbksh ""
    stderr_zbksh "Usage: ${1##*/} [-?vV] [-u] [-l]"
    stderr_zbksh ""
    stderr_zbksh "  Where:"
    stderr_zbksh "    -u = Convert command line arguments to upper case"
    stderr_zbksh "    -l = Convert command line arguments to lower case"
    stderr_zbksh "    -v = Verbose mode - displays function info"
    stderr_zbksh "    -V = Very Verbose Mode - debug output displayed"
    stderr_zbksh "    -? = Help - display this message"
    stderr_zbksh ""
    stderr_zbksh "Author: Your Name (YourEmail@address.com)"
    stderr_zbksh ""
    stderr_zbksh "\"AutoContent\" enabled"
    stderr_zbksh "\"Multi-Shell\" enabled"
    stderr_zbksh ""
}
```

In the Library template version, a couple of variables are no longer required, and a new library function is added:

- Removed ${GBL_ECHO}

- Removed ${CMD_ECHO}

- Added stderr_zbksh

The command "stderr_zbksh" is called from a remote function library whose action is easy to guess. It displays its command line arguments on the Standard Error stream, i.e., file descriptor "2". So the "usagemsg_my_template03_zbksh" function does not contain any "echo", "print", or "printf" commands. All output is performed externally using library functions. The actual content of the usage message is unchanged, only the mechanism for displaying the content is different.

The next section from the Library template is the same as in the Intermediate and Basic templates, which is the documentation area:

```
##################################################
####
#### Description:
####
#### Place a full text description of your shell function here.
####
#### Assumptions:
####
#### Provide a list of assumptions your shell function makes,
#### with a description of each assumption.
####
#### Dependencies:
####
#### Provide a list of dependencies your shell function has,
#### with a description of each dependency.
####
#### Products:
####
#### Provide a list of output your shell function produces,
#### with a description of each product.
####
#### Configured Usage:
####
#### Describe how your shell function should be used.
####
#### Details:
####
#### Place nothing here, the details are your shell function.
####
##################################################
```

Again, we will dispense with a detailed description of this section.

Next, the "configure_my_template03_zbksh" function. The difference between the Intermediate and Library versions is the removal of the "CMD_ECHO" variable and the use of the "stderr_zbksh" external library function.

Intermediate Template Configuration Function:

```
configure_my_template02_zbksh()
```

```
{
####
#### Notice this function is a POSIX function so that it can see local
#### and global variables from calling functions and scripts.
####
#### Configuration parameters can be stored in a file and
#### this script can be dynamically reconfigured by sending
#### the running script a HUP signal using the kill command.
####
#### Configuration variables can be defined in the configuration file using
#### the same syntax as defining a shell variable, e.g.: VARIABLE="value"

    CMD_ECHO="${GBL_ECHO:-echo -e }"

    [[ "_${1}" != "_" ]] && MYT_CFILE=~/.${1}.conf

    (( VERBOSE == TRUE )) && ${CMD_ECHO} "# Configuration File: ${MYT_CFILE}"

    if [[ -f ${MYT_CFILE} ]]
    then
        (( VERBOSE == TRUE )) && cat ${MYT_CFILE}
        . ${MYT_CFILE}
    fi

    return 0
}
```

The Library Template Configuration Function:

```
configure_my_template03_zbksh()
{
####
#### Notice this function is a POSIX function so that it can see local
#### and global variables from calling functions and scripts.
####
#### Configuration parameters can be stored in a file and
#### this script can be dynamically reconfigured by sending
#### the running script a HUP signal using the kill command.
####
#### Configuration variables can be defined in the configuration file using
#### the same syntax as defining a shell variable, e.g.: VARIABLE="value"

    [[ "_${1}" != "_" ]] && MYT_CFILE=~/.${1}.conf

    (( VERBOSE == TRUE )) && stderr_zbksh "# Configuration File:
${MYT_CFILE}"

    if [[ -f ${MYT_CFILE} ]]
    then
        (( VERBOSE == TRUE )) && cat ${MYT_CFILE}
        . ${MYT_CFILE}
    fi

    return 0
}
```

This small change allows the code to be operable in multiple shell script
interpreters by removing any shell specific commands from the function.

The purpose of the configuration function remains unchanged from the
Intermediate and Basic templates, which is to provide a dynamic
mechanism of configuring the shell script function. It executes a
configuration file which is assumed to contain shell code. Usually this file

contains shell variable definitions, however it may contain any shell code desired, including references to outside functions, applications, or utilities.

Again, this Library template configuration function contains embedded documentation identified as comments beginning with 4 #'s followed by a space.

The next section of the Library template script contains the commands that are to be executed as the primary action of the script. This is a function named "my_template03_zbksh" and the function declaration is defined using the Korn Shell style definition syntax. One of the features of using this syntax is the function programmer has the ability to assign local variables inside the function. However if this same script is executed as a Bash script, all variables become global variables regardless of the function definition syntax or use of the "typeset" built-in command.

It is normally best practice to initialize all local variables at the beginning of each function, however some shell interpreters do not support local variable definitions. To accommodate these shell interpreters, it is best to use variable names that are unique to each function for local variables. This can be observed in the variable initialization section of the "my_template03_zbksh" function:

```
typeset TRUE="${TRUE:-0}"
typeset FALSE="${FALSE:-1}"
typeset VERBOSE="${VERBOSE:-${FALSE}}"
typeset VERYVERB="${VERYVERB:-${FALSE}}"
typeset OPTIND="1"
typeset MYT_PROGRAM="my_template03_zbksh"
typeset MYT_VERSION="1.0"
typeset MYT_TGGLEUP="${FALSE}"
typeset MYT_TGGLELO="${FALSE}"
typeset MYT_ARGVALU=""
```

Observe in the Library Template version of this function, the "CMD_ECHO" variable is no longer defined, and is no longer needed in the function. These mechanisms now exist in external library functions.

Much of the same logic applies to the Library Template function as the Intermediate version, but it is worth repeating here to drive home these points:

- The global variables have common names that are used in every script where the variable is needed. The local variables in this instance all begin with the prefix "MYT_". The variable prefix should be unique and different to each function. This practice will reduce the possibility of errors when executing this script between multiple shells where local variables may not be supported.

- The "OPTIND" variable is used with the "getopts" function to reference the last command line option processed. An anomaly of a shell interpreter that does not support local variables, such as Bash, is if a function is called from another function while processing command line options, the value of the OPTIND variable will be corrupted in the called function. To avoid this issue, it is recommended that the OPTIND variable be initialized at the beginning of any function using the "getopts" function.

Next, the configuration function is called and executed to dynamically reconfigure any variables hardcoded into the variable initialization section.

```
#### Call the configuration function and execute the configuration file.
configure_my_template03_zbksh "${MYT_PROGRAM}"
```

Notice the first command line parameter is the local variable MYT_PROGRAM which contains the name of the Library template function.

The command line option processing section of the Library template is identical to the Intermediate template function, so a detailed discussion will be skipped.

```
#### Process the command line options and arguments.
while getopts ":vvul" OPTION
do
  case "${OPTION}" in
    'u') MYT_TGGLEUP="${TRUE}";;
    'l') MYT_TGGLELO="${TRUE}";;
    'v') VERBOSE="${TRUE}";;
    'V') VERYVERB="${TRUE}";;
    '?') usagemsg_my_template03_zbksh "${MYT_PROGRAM}" "${MYT_VERSION}" &&
return 1 ;;
    ':') usagemsg_my_template03_zbksh "${MYT_PROGRAM}" "${MYT_VERSION}" &&
return 2 ;;
    '#') usagemsg_my_template03_zbksh "${MYT_PROGRAM}" "${MYT_VERSION}" &&
return 3 ;;
  esac
done

shift $(( ${OPTIND} - 1 ))
```

If you would like to review a detailed discussion of the above section of code, see the previous chapter.

Previously, in the Intermediate template, the error checking section of code displayed error messages using the command specified by the value of the "CMD_ECHO" variable. In the Library template version, the error messages are displayed using the external library function named "stderr_zbksh".

```
##################################################
#### Place any command line option error checking statements
#### here.  If an error is detected, print a message to
#### standard error, and return from this function with a
#### non-zero return code.  The "trap" statement will cause
#### the "usagemsg" to be displayed.
        trap "usagemsg_my_template03_zbksh ${MYT_PROGRAM} ${MYT_VERSION}" EXIT

        if (( MYT_TGGLEUP == TRUE )) &&
           (( MYT_TGGLELO == TRUE ))
        then
            stderr_zbksh "# ERROR: Do not specify both upper and lower case
conversion together"
            return 11
        fi

        trap "-" EXIT

##################################################
```

Other than the change in display mechanisms, the error processing code is the same between the Intermediate and Library template versions.

> **NOTE: Much of the logic detail is being skipped in this chapter because it has been covered in the previous chapter. The primary logic differences between the Intermediate and Library templates are the output mechanisms. Since the logic was discussed in the previous chapter, this chapter focuses on the externalized output mechanism and skips repeating much of the logic discussion.**

The next section of code displays the values of the configuration options, variables, and settings. The differences shown here are again the output mechanisms: external library functions are used here instead of the "CMD_ECHO" variable:

```
##################################################
        (( VERYVERB == TRUE )) && set -x
        (( VERBOSE  == TRUE )) && stderr_zbksh "# Program Name..........:
${MYT_PROGRAM}"
        (( VERBOSE  == TRUE )) && stderr_zbksh "# Version...............:
${MYT_VERSION}"

        for MYT_ARGVALU in "${@}"
```

```
        do
            (( VERBOSE == TRUE )) && stderr_zbksh "# Command Line Arg......:
${MYT_ARGVALU}"
        done

    ##################################################
```

As much or as little information can be displayed here, it is up to the function programmer to determine what information would be valuable to the script programmer or user if they specified VERBOSE mode.

Finally we get to the primary action of the script function, which is identical to the Intermediate script, except the output display functions called from the external function library.

```
    if (( ${#@} > 0 ))
    then
        MYT_MSG="${@}"
    fi

    if [[ "_${MYT_MSG}" != "_" ]]
    then
        (( MYT_TGGLEUP == TRUE )) && typeset -u MYT_MSG="${MYT_MSG}"
        (( MYT_TGGLELO == TRUE )) && typeset -l MYT_MSG="${MYT_MSG}"

        (( VERBOSE == TRUE )) && stderr_zbksh "# MYT_MSG Variable Value:
${MYT_MSG}"
        stdout_zbksh "${MYT_MSG}"
    fi
```

However observe that a new external library function is being called and is named "stdout_zbksh". It displays command line arguments on the Standard Output stream, i.e., file descriptor "1".

The last statement of the function "my_template03_zbksh" is to return with a zero (0) or TRUE return code to the calling function or script. In this instance it would return to the main body of the script and since it was the last statement of the script, it would then exit to the calling shell.

At this time, the reader may want to copy the content of the Library template from Appendix C to a file on your UNIX/Linux/Cygwin desktop for testing and reference.

The actual testing of this script will be deferred until the end of the next chapter. The reason to delay the testing is because the script just examined uses external library functions, therefore a discussion of the external library functions is required before testing is performed. The next chapter is that discussion.

Chapter 5: Create a Function Library

This chapter will discuss how to create a function library and the advanced functions in the library. A Shell Script Function Library is a reusable source of functions, routines, and procedures which can be utilized by the shell script programmer.

There is an instructional video titled "How to Create a Shell Script Function Library" available at:

http://www.mtxia.com/js/Downloads/adv_part01

Shell Script Function Libraries provide the following features and benefits:

- Maintenance and updates of the functions in the library are easier. And that is because they only need to be performed in a single file, instead of updating each standalone script that includes the function.

- Another advantage is it saves memory. Functions are loaded only when they are needed and many scripts can use a library function simultaneously.

- Saves disk space. Many scripts can share a single copy of a library function on disk.

- But certainly, the biggest advantage of a Shell Script Function Library is standardization of code. Every shell script that utilizes the library calls the same functions from the same library.

The first step in creating a function library is to create a directory to contain the functions. This directory can exist anywhere, for example: each user can have their own function library. But if the functions are to be shared between multiple users, a centralized location may be desirable, such as "/usr/local/functions."

For the purpose of this book and discussion, we will create a directory called "functions/adv_zbksh" for the library under the home of the current user.

```
mkdir -p ~/functions/adv_zbksh
chmod -R 755 ~/functions
```

Now create the functions in the function library. Copy each function into a file under the function library directory with a file name matching the function name. If more than one function is in the file, copy it for each function, naming each file according to the function names.

For example, assume there is a standalone shell script called "echo_zbksh" which contains the following three functions:

- function echo_zbksh

- function stdout_zbksh

- function stderr_zbksh

Copy the standalone script file into the function library directory, once for each function in the script:

```
cp echo_zbksh ~/functions/adv_zbksh/echo_zbksh
cp echo_zbksh ~/functions/adv_zbksh/stdout_zbksh
cp echo_zbksh ~/functions/adv_zbksh/stderr_zbksh
```

Now edit each of the files in the function library and remove everything from the file except the function matching the file name. When finished, each file should contain one function and the function name should match the file name and the function declaration should be on the first line of the file. To restate this point: the function name should match the file name and each file should contain one function.

```
vi ~/functions/adv_zbksh/echo_zbksh
vi ~/functions/adv_zbksh/stdout_zbksh
vi ~/functions/adv_zbksh/stderr_zbksh
```

The "function" declaration line needs to be the first line in each file, and the SHEBANG line "#!/..." should be removed.

Now the functions are ready to be called from any shell script by any user, assuming the function directory is accessible and the function files are readable by any user.

In the new shell script being written, reference the function library using the "FPATH" environment variable, for example:

```
#!/usr/bin/ksh93
FPATH=~/functions/adv_zbksh
export FPATH
```

The FPATH variable is used just like the normal PATH variable, so multiple function libraries can be listed, separated by a colon ":" delimiter, for example:

```
#!/usr/bin/ksh93
FPATH=~/functions/adv_zbksh:/usr/local/functions
export FPATH
```

When this script is interpreted by Korn Shell, the directories in the FPATH variable are searched for functions with matching names when a command is executed in a shell script, and the first match is loaded into memory and executed.

In other shell script interpreters, the FPATH variable may or may not be recognized, so a different mechanism will be used to search for matching function names. In order to standardize the use of the FPATH variable for function libraries, it is necessary to provide a search mechanism for those shell script interpreters that do not current use the FPATH variable. Such a mechanism is shown below:

```
    #### Loop thru each directory in the FPATH list using a colon (:)
delimiter.
    #### Process each directory in reverse order to simulate results of
    #### searching the FPATH directory.

    IFS=":"
    FDIRS=( ${FPATH} )
    IFS=$' \t\n'

    END=${#FDIRS[@]}
    for (( IDX=END-1; IDX>=0; --IDX ))
    do
        FDIR="${FDIRS[${IDX}]}"

    #### Gather a list of functions ending in *_zbksh from the directory and
loop
    #### thru each file using a "for"loop.

        for FUNC in ${FDIR}/*_zbksh
            do
    ####
    #### Check each *_zbksh file to see if it starts with a function, if so
    #### cache it in the current environment by running it as as a "dot"
script.
    ####
            if head -1 "${FUNC}" 2>/dev/null | egrep 'function|\(\)' > /dev/null
2>&1
            then
                . "${FUNC}"
            fi
        done
    done
```

As described in the previous chapter, the above code searches each directory for defined functions and then loads each function into memory.

By doing this, whenever a function is called from a shell script, it is already in memory and will be executed. The above code gathers a list of all files in each directory that end with the suffix "_zbksh" and then checks to see if the first line of each file contains the string "function" or a pair of parenthesis "()". If so, the file is assumed to be a compatible shell script function and it is loaded into memory as a "dot" script.

Although the above code does not exactly match the Korn Shell behavior when processing the FPATH variable, it does provide an adequate result for Bash or Zshell. All the functions defined in the FPATH directories are cached and available to be called by the primary shell script. This code will be externalized to a generic "dot" script in a later chapter.

With regard to the functions discussed in this book, the full source code for each function is defined in Appendix D and is available for download at:

http://www.mtxia.com/js/Downloads/adv_part01

These functions include:

- append_string_zbksh

- check_dns_zbksh

- check_port_zbksh

- configure_zbksh

- echo_zbksh

- execl_zbksh

- find_dot_file_zbksh

- mkewuid_zbksh

- randomize_array_zbksh

- random_string_zbksh

- sort_array_zbksh

- stderr_comment_zbksh

- stderr_zbksh

- stdout_zbksh

- transpose_filter_zbksh

- trap_zbksh

- usagemsg_zbksh

- verbose_comment_zbksh

- wikiAutoLoad_zbksh

If you download the "tar.gz" file from
http://www.mtxia.com/js/Downloads/adv_part01/adv_zbksh.tar.gz you
will see numerous files that are not functions. These include several
standalone shell scripts which are described and used as examples in this
book. You will also see numerous hidden files(beginning with a dot ".").
These hidden files will be discussed in the chapter titled "Automated
Documentation".

It is recommended that you download the "tar.gz" file from
http://www.mtxia.com/js/Downloads/adv_part01/adv_zbksh.tar.gz and
extract that file into a directory under your home directory named as
follows:

```
mkdir -p ~/functions/adv_zbksh
mv   "adv_zbksh.tar.gz"  ~/functions/adv_zbksh
cd   ~/functions/adv_zbksh
gzip -cd adv_zbksh.tar.gz | tar -tvf -
```

If you choose not to download the "tar.gz" file, then create each of the
functions by copy-and-paste from Appendix D. These functions will be
necessary for all the examples and demonstrations provided in the
remainder of this book.

After the shell script function library "adv_zbksh" has been created, any
of the functions in the library may be called from any shell script.

In the previous chapter, we deferred testing the shell script named
"my_template03_zbksh" because it called functions from the
"adv_zbksh" function library. Once the function library has been created,

you may proceed with testing the "my_template03_zbksh" script. This testing may be performed now assuming the standalone shell script .containing the Library Function template has 755 (rwxr-xr-x) permissions.

In this first script execution, run the script as a "ksh93" script. Edit the script and specify the full path file name of the Korn Shell 93 interpreter as the SHEBANG line:

```
#!/usr/bin/ksh93
#!/bin/bash
#!/bin/zsh
##################################################
####
#### This script will run in KornShell93, Zshell, or Bash, all you need to do
#### is put the desired "shebang" line at the top of the script.
####
##################################################
```

Then run the following script:

```
$ ./my_template03_zbksh
$
```

Since there were no command line arguments, nothing was displayed. Run it again with the "-?" command line argument to cause it to display the usage message:

```
$ ./my_template03_zbksh -?

Program: my_template03_zbksh          Version: 1.0

Place a brief description ( < 255 chars ) of your shell
function here.

Usage: my_template03_zbksh [-?vV] [-u] [-l]

    Where:
      -u = Convert command line arguments to upper case
      -l = Convert command line arguments to lower case
      -v = Verbose mode - displays my_template02_zbksh function info
      -V = Very Verbose Mode - debug output displayed
      -? = Help - display this message

Author: Your Name (YourEmail@address.com)

"AutoContent" enabled
"Multi-Shell" enabled

$
```

If you review the code in "my_template03_zbksh" you will see the usage message is being displayed by calling a library function called "stderr_zbksh". This function sends its output to standard error

(STDERR), not standard output (STDOUT). So to prove it is calling the library function "stderr_zbksh", run it again and redirect STDERR to "/dev/null".

```
$ ./my_template03_zbksh -? 2>/dev/null
```

The usage message should not be displayed, because the "stderr_zbksh" library function displays its output on STDERR, and STDERR was redirected to "/dev/null"

Edit the configuration file and add a default value for the variable "MYT_MSG".

```
vi ~/my_template03_zbksh.conf
MYT_MSG="Hello World!"
:wq
```

Then run the script again with no command line arguments:

```
$ ./my_template03_zbksh
Hello World!
```

Review the source code for the shell script "my_template03_zbksh" and see the script is calling the library function "stdout_zbksh", which sends its output to STDOUT. To prove this, run the script again and redirect STDOUT to a temporary file, then view the contents of the temporary file.

```
$ ./my_template03_zbksh > /tmp/tmp.out
$ cat /tmp/tmp.out
Hello World!
```

The contents of the file "/tmp/tmp.out" should now contain the output from the script execution.

Re-run the script using the upper and lower case options to prove the script works the same as seen in a previous chapter, the difference now is the script is calling external functions from the function library.

```
$ ./my_template03_zbksh -u
HELLO WORLD!

$ ./my_template03_zbksh -l
hello world!

$ ./my_template03_zbksh -u -l
# ERROR: Do not specify both upper and lower case conversion together

Program: my_template03_zbksh          Version: 1.0
```

```
Place a brief description ( < 255 chars ) of your shell
function here.

Usage: my_template03_zbksh [-?vV] [-u] [-l]

   where:
     -u = Convert command line arguments to upper case
     -l = Convert command line arguments to lower case
     -v = Verbose mode - displays my_template02_zbksh function info
     -V = Very Verbose Mode - debug output displayed
     -? = Help - display this message

Author: Your Name (YourEmail@address.com)

"AutoContent" enabled
"Multi-Shell" enabled

$
```

Change the SHEBANG line to bash, and re-run the script commands.
This will cause the script to cache the library functions in memory and call
them as needed. The results should be the same as seen previously.

```
vi my_template03_zbksh
#!/bin/bash
#!/usr/bin/ksh93
#!/bin/zsh
##################################################
####
#### This script will run in KornShell93, Zshell, or Bash, all you need to
do
#### is put the desired "shebang" line at the top of the script.
####
##################################################
...
...
...
:wq


$ ./my_template03_zbksh -u
HELLO WORLD!

$ ./my_template03_zbksh -l
hello world!

$ ./my_template03_zbksh -u -l
# ERROR: Do not specify both upper and lower case conversion together

Program: my_template03_zbksh          Version: 1.0

Place a brief description ( < 255 chars ) of your shell
function here.

Usage: my_template03_zbksh [-?vV] [-u] [-l]

   where:
     -u = Convert command line arguments to upper case
     -l = Convert command line arguments to lower case
     -v = Verbose mode - displays my_template02_zbksh function info
     -V = Very Verbose Mode - debug output displayed
     -? = Help - display this message

Author: Your Name (YourEmail@address.com)

"AutoContent" enabled
"Multi-Shell" enabled
```

Re-run the script as many times as you want, changing the SHEBANG line for each new shell interpreter you want to test. Use the "-v" and "-V" options to display the VERBOSE and VERYVERB output.

In this examination of the Library template it is seen that shell scripts can dynamically call external functions from a function library, even when executed by shell interpreters that do not natively support the FPATH variable.

The next chapter will define and examine the Advanced Shell Script Template.

Chapter 6: The Advanced Template

All of the necessary components are now identified and defined that are necessary to create the Advanced Template Shell Script. Initially it will be presented as a standalone script containing all needed functions within itself. Then it will be presented with all functions externalized and called from a standalone script. Additional functions will be introduced which support automated documentation where the usage message hidden documentation file will be examined.

View the Advanced Template contained in Appendix E.

The new library functions introduced in this chapter include the following:

- find_dot_file_zbksh

    o   Uses Korn Shell Style function definition

    o   Displays a usage message to standard output

- my_template04_zbksh

    o   Uses Korn Shell style function definition

    o   Primary activities performed here

- Main body of the standalone script

    o   Multi-Shell setup and configuration

    o   Function Libraries setup and configuration

In the Advanced Template, the purpose is to bring together all the concepts discussed so far into a reusable template. The primary difference between the Advanced Template and the previous templates, is the introduction of the function "find_dot_file_zbksh". This function searches the directories identified in the FPATH variable for hidden files corresponding to configuration files, usage message files, documentation, and example execution output. This function simplifies the implementation of automated documentation, which will be discussed in the next chapter.

The standardized format of a shell script function should be familiar to the reader by now, it starts with the function declaration, followed by the variable initialization section:

```
find_dot_file_zbksh()
#### #############################################
{
   typeset DOT_PROGRAM="find_dot_file_zbksh"
   typeset DOT_VERSION="1.0"
   typeset DOT_TRUE="0"
   typeset DOT_FALSE="1"
   typeset DOT_VERBOSE="${DOT_VERBOSE:-${DOT_FALSE}}"
   typeset DOT_VERYVERB="${DOT_VERYVERB:-${DOT_FALSE}}"
   typeset OPTIND="1"
   typeset DOT_FUNCNAME="find_dot_file_zbksh"
   typeset DOT_ACTION="usagemsg"
   typeset DOT_EXTFILE="./.find_dot_file_zbksh.usagemsg"
   typeset DOT_RETCODE="99"
   typeset DOT_DIR
   typeset DOT_LINE
   typeset DOT_RECURS="${DOT_RECURS:-${TRUE}}"

#################################################
```

In order to prevent unlimited recursion when this functions calls itself for configuration and documentation files, a test has been added to stop recursion after the first iteration.

```
#################################################
   if (( DOT_RECURS == DOT_TRUE ))
   then
       DOT_RECURS="${DOT_FALSE}"
       find_dot_file_zbksh -f "find_dot_file_zbksh" -a "configure"
   else
       DOT_RECURS="${DOT_TRUE}"
       return 0
   fi
#################################################
```

There is of course the "getopts" section where the command line options are processed. The options to this function allow the user to specify a function name and action to perform. The function name will normally correspond to the current function name (but does not have to do so), the "action" directs the function to process a hidden file in a specific way such as "configuration", "usagemsg", "document", "example", or other actions defined by the function/script programmer. New actions should be added to the "find_dot_files_zbksh" function as needed.

```
#################################################
####
#### Process the command line options and arguments, saving
#### the values as appropriate.
####
```

```
          while getopts ":vVDEf:a:" OPTION
          do
             DOT_OPTIND="${OPTIND}"
             case "${OPTION}" in
                'f') DOT_FUNCNAME="${OPTARG}";;
                'a') DOT_ACTION="${OPTARG}";;
                'v') DOT_VERBOSE="${DOT_TRUE}";;
                'V') DOT_VERYVERB="${DOT_TRUE}";;
                'D') find_dot_file_zbksh -f "${DOT_PROGRAM}" -a "document" && return
4;;
                'E') find_dot_file_zbksh -f "${DOT_PROGRAM}" -a "example" && return
5;;
                '?') find_dot_file_zbksh -f "${DOT_PROGRAM}" -a "usagemsg" && return
1 ;;
                ':') find_dot_file_zbksh -f "${DOT_PROGRAM}" -a "usagemsg" && return
2 ;;
                '#') find_dot_file_zbksh -f "${DOT_PROGRAM}" -a "usagemsg" && return
3 ;;
             esac
             OPTIND="${DOT_OPTIND}"
          done

          shift $(( ${OPTIND} - 1 ))

          (( DOT_VERYVERB == DOT_TRUE )) && set -x

          ##################################################
```

The option verification section tests the user specified command line
arguments to verify they conform to acceptable values. In this version of
the function, the "action" specified by the script programmer must be one
of the following literal values (upper or lower case):

- configure

- usagemsg

- document

- example

```
          ##################################################
          ####
          #### Check the command line arguments to verify they are valid values and
that all
          #### necessary information was specified.
          ####

          #    trap "find_dot_file_zbksh -f find_dot_file_zbksh -a usagemsg" EXIT

          if [[ "_${DOT_FUNCNAME}" == "_" ]]
          then
          #        verbose_comment_zbksh -v "${DOT_VERBOSE}" -c "ERROR: Function Name
not specified"
                 return 10
          fi

          if [[ "_${DOT_ACTION}" != _[Cc][Oo][Nn][Ff][Ii][Gg][Uu][Rr][Ee] ]] &&
             [[ "_${DOT_ACTION}" != _[Uu][Ss][Aa][Gg][Ee][Mm][Ss][Gg]      ]] &&
             [[ "_${DOT_ACTION}" == _[Dd][Oo][Cc][Uu][Mm][Ee][Nn][Tt]      ]] &&
             [[ "_${DOT_ACTION}" == _[Ee][Xx][Aa][Mm][Pp][Ll][Ee]          ]]
          then
```

```
        stderr_comment_zbksh -p "ERROR: Invalid Action Specified" -a
"${DOT_ACTION}"
        find_dot_file_zbksh -f "find_dot_file_zbksh" -a "usagemsg"
        return 11
    fi

#    trap "-" EXIT

###################################################
```

As seen in previous templates, the "usagemsg_zbksh" function has been replaced in the Advanced template with the "find_dot_file_zbksh" function. This function is used to display the usage message by specifying the command line options "-f find_dot_file_zbksh" and "-a usagemsg". These options instruct the function to search the directories specified in the FPATH variable for a hidden file (a file beginning with a dot) named ".find_dot_file_zbksh.usagemsg" and then displays its contents on the Standard Error (STDERR) stream.

The next section of the "find_dot_file_zbksh" function displays the function information and command line argument values specified by the script programmer or user; this section should already be familiar to the reader.

```
    ###################################################

    ####
    #### Display some DOT_PROGRAM info and the command line arguments specified
    #### if "DOT_VERBOSE" mode was specified.
    ####

    (( DOT_VERYVERB == DOT_TRUE )) && set -x
    verbose_comment_zbksh -v "${DOT_VERBOSE}" -p "Program"          -a
"${DOT_PROGRAM}"
    verbose_comment_zbksh -v "${DOT_VERBOSE}" -p "Version"          -a
"${DOT_VERSION}"
    verbose_comment_zbksh -v "${DOT_VERBOSE}" -p "Function Name"    -a
"${DOT_FUNCNAME}"
    verbose_comment_zbksh -v "${DOT_VERBOSE}" -p "Action"           -a
"${DOT_ACTION}"

    ###################################################
    ####
    ####
    ####

    DOT_RETCODE="0"

    ###################################################
```

The directory contents of the FPATH variable is separated into an array and searched for hidden files in the order in which the directories appear in the FPATH variable.

```
    ###################################################
```

```
#### Define the possible directory locations for the "dot" files in the
FPATH directories.

    IDX="0"
    IFS=$': \t\n'
    for DIR in ${FPATH}
    do
        DOT_FPATHS[IDX++]="${DIR}"
    done
    IFS=$' \t\n'

    ##################################################
```

Additional directories are added to the search list and can be modified by
the script programmer as necessary or desired.

```
    ##################################################

    #### Define the possible directory locations for the "dot" files under the
    users HOME.

    ####    typeset DOT_HOMES[0]=~
    ####    typeset DOT_HOMES[1]=~/.adv_zbksh
    ####    typeset DOT_HOMES[2]=~/adv_zbksh
    ####    typeset DOT_HOMES[3]=~/functions/adv_zbksh
    ####    typeset DOT_HOMES[4]=~/functions

      IDX="0"
      DOT_HOMES[IDX++]=~
      DOT_HOMES[IDX++]=~/.adv_zbksh
      DOT_HOMES[IDX++]=~/adv_zbksh
      DOT_HOMES[IDX++]=~/functions/adv_zbksh
      DOT_HOMES[IDX++]=~/functions

    #### Define the possible directory locations for the "dot" files under
    /usr/local.

    ####    typeset DOT_LOCALS[0]="/usr/local/adv_zbksh"
    ####    typeset DOT_LOCALS[1]="/usr/local/functions/adv_zbksh"
    ####    typeset DOT_LOCALS[2]="/usr/local/functions"
    ####    typeset DOT_LOCALS[3]="/usr/local/scripts/adv_zbksh"
    ####    typeset DOT_LOCALS[4]="/usr/local/scripts"

      IDX="0"
      DOT_LOCALS[IDX++]="/usr/local/adv_zbksh"
      DOT_LOCALS[IDX++]="/usr/local/functions/adv_zbksh"
      DOT_LOCALS[IDX++]="/usr/local/functions"
      DOT_LOCALS[IDX++]="/usr/local/scripts/adv_zbksh"
      DOT_LOCALS[IDX++]="/usr/local/scripts"

    #### Define the possible directory locations for the "dot" files under MAN
    pages.

    ####    typeset DOT_MANS[0]="/usr/share/man/man1"
      IDX="0"
      DOT_MANS[IDX++]="/usr/share/man/man1"

    #### Define the "dot" file name extensions based on the CLI action
    specified.

        [[ "_${DOT_ACTION}" == _[Cc][Oo][Nn][Ff][Ii][Gg][Uu][Rr][Ee] ]] &&
    DOT_EXTENSION=".conf"
        [[ "_${DOT_ACTION}" == _[Uu][Ss][Aa][Gg][Ee][Mm][Ss][Gg]     ]] &&
    DOT_EXTENSION=".usagemsg"
        [[ "_${DOT_ACTION}" == _[Dd][Oo][Cc][Uu][Mm][Ee][Nn][Tt]     ]] &&
    DOT_EXTENSION=".usagemsg"
        [[ "_${DOT_ACTION}" == _[Ee][Xx][Aa][Mm][Pp][Ll][Ee]         ]] &&
    DOT_EXTENSION=".usagemsg"
```

```
        #    verbose_comment_zbksh -v "${DOT_VERBOSE}" -p "File Extension" -a
    "${DOT_EXTENSION}"

        #### Loop through each of the directory locations searching for the first
    occurrence of
        #### a matching "dot" file. The directories are search in order of HOMES,
    LOCALS, MANS.
        #### The first "dot" file found cause the loop to break.

        for DOT_DIR in "${DOT_FPATHS[@]}" "${DOT_HOMES[@]}" "${DOT_LOCALS[@]}"
    "${DOT_MANS[@]}"
        do
            if [[ -f "${DOT_DIR}/.${DOT_FUNCNAME}${DOT_EXTENSION}" ]]
            then
                DOT_EXTFILE="${DOT_DIR}/.${DOT_FUNCNAME}${DOT_EXTENSION}"
        #        verbose_comment_zbksh -v "${DOT_VERBOSE}" -p "External File Found"
    -a "${DOT_EXTFILE}"
                break
            fi
        done
```

If the user specified the command line "action" argument as the literal
value of "configure", then execute the hidden file corresponding with the
function name and extension ".conf" (${DOT_EXTFILE}) as a "dot"
script in the current shell environment.

```
        #### If an external dot file exists, and the action is "configure", then
        #### execute the file as a "dot" script in the current environment
        if [[    "_${DOT_EXTFILE}" != "_"          ]] &&
           [[    "_${DOT_EXTFILE}" == _*.conf       ]] &&
           [[ -f "${DOT_EXTFILE}"                   ]] &&
           [[    "_${DOT_ACTION}"  == _[Cc][Oo][Nn][Ff][Ii][Gg][Uu][Rr][Ee] ]]
        then
            . ${DOT_EXTFILE}
        #        verbose_comment_zbksh -v "${DOT_VERBOSE}" -p "Executing dot script"
    -a "${DOT_EXTFILE}"
        fi
```

If the user specified command line "action" argument is the literal value
of "usagemsg", then read each line of the hidden file corresponding with
the function name and extension ".usagemsg" (${DOT_EXTFILE}) and
display the contents on Standard Error (STDERR).

```
        #### If an external dot file exists, and the action is "usagemsg", then
        #### display the file on STDERR as a usage message.
        if [[    "_${DOT_EXTFILE}" != "_"          ]] &&
           [[    "_${DOT_EXTFILE}" == _*.usagemsg   ]] &&
           [[ -f "${DOT_EXTFILE}"                   ]] &&
           [[    "_${DOT_ACTION}"  == _[Uu][Ss][Aa][Gg][Ee][Mm][Ss][Gg]      ]]
        then
        #        verbose_comment_zbksh -v "${DOT_VERBOSE}" -p "Displaying dot
    script" -a "${DOT_EXTFILE}"
            while IFS="" read -r -- DOT_LINE
            do
                stderr_zbksh -- "${DOT_LINE}"
            done < "${DOT_EXTFILE}"
        fi
```

If the user specified command line "action" argument is the literal value of "document", then read each line of the hidden file corresponding with the function name and extension ".usagemsg" (${DOT_EXTFILE}) and display the contents on Standard Output (STDOUT). Also extract the comments from the user specified function itself, and display those on STDOUT too.

```
#### If an external dot file exists, and the action is "document", then
#### display usagemsg, comments, and examples on STDOUT.
  if [[     "_${DOT_EXTFILE}" != "_" ]] &&
     [[     "_${DOT_EXTFILE}" == _*.usagemsg ]] &&
     [[  -f "${DOT_EXTFILE}"              ]] &&
     [[     "_${DOT_ACTION}"  == _[Dd][Oo][Cc][Uu][Mm][Ee][Nn][Tt]    ]]
  then
      while IFS="" read -r -- DOT_LINE
      do
          stdout_zbksh -- "${DOT_LINE}"
      done < "${DOT_EXTFILE}"

      grep '^#### ' ${DOT_FUNCNAME} | sed -e 's/^#### //g'
  fi
```

If the user specified command line "action" argument is the literal value of "example", then extract the lines of text from the "usagemsg" file (${DOT_EXTFILE}) and execute each example. Capture the results from each example and display them on Standard Output (STDOUT).

```
#### If an external dot file exists, and the action is "example", then
#### execute the function examples and display the results on STDOUT.
  if    [[     "_${DOT_EXTFILE}" != "_" ]] &&
        [[  -f "${DOT_EXTFILE}"         ]] &&
      ( [[     "_${DOT_ACTION}"  == _[Dd][Oo][Cc][Uu][Mm][Ee][Nn][Tt] ]] ||
        [[     "_${DOT_ACTION}"  == _[Ee][Xx][Aa][Mm][Pp][Ll][Ee]     ]] )
  then
      IFS=$'\n'

      sed -e '/Example Usage:/,/^$/ !d' ${DOT_EXTFILE} >
/tmp/tmp${$}.example
      IDX=0
      while read LINE
      do
          DOT_EXAMPLES[IDX++]="${LINE}"
      done < /tmp/tmp${$}.example
      rm -f /tmp/tmp${$}.example
      DOT_EXAMPLES[0]=''

      IFS=$' \t\n'

      for DOT_EXAMPLE in "${DOT_EXAMPLES[@]}"
      do
          [[ "_${DOT_EXAMPLE}" == "_" ]] && continue
          [[ "_${SHCODE}" == "_korn" ]] && set -x
              eval ${DOT_EXAMPLE}
          [[ "_${SHCODE}" == "_korn" ]] && set +x
      done
  fi

  OPTIND="1"

  return 0
```

```
}
####
#### ##################################################
```

The changes associated with the Advanced Template can be seen in the
"my_template04_zbksh" function. These script changes implement the
"find_dot_file_zbksh" function to locate and execute the configuration
file:

```
...
...
... typeset MYT_PROGRAM="my_template04_zbksh"
...
...
... find_dot_file_zbksh -f "${MYT_PROGRAM}" -a "configure"
```

The above command will cause the function to search the directories in
the FPATH variable for a hidden configuration file named
".my_template04_zbksh.conf".

The ".my_template04_zbksh.conf" configuration file should be located in
the same directory as the "my_template04_zbksh" function and has the
following contents:

```
##################################################
####
#### This is the configuration file for the program "my_template04_zbksh".
The
#### values show below are the default values for each configurable
variable.
#### If you want to change a value, copy the configuration line, uncomment
#### it, and change the value.
####
##################################################
# MYT_PROGRAM="my_template04_zbksh"

# VERSION="1.0"

MYT_MSG="Hello World!"
```

This configuration file is executed as a "dot" script in the current shell
environment, which has the effect of initializing the "MYT_MSG" shell
variable with a value of "Hello World!".

The "find_dot_file_zbksh" function is also used as a replacement for all
"usagemsg" function calls, such as is seen in the "getopts" section of
code:

```
#### Process the command line options and arguments.
    OPTIND="1"
```

```
while getopts ":vVulDE" OPTION
do
    case "${OPTION}" in
        'u') MYT_TGGLEUP="${TRUE}";;
        'l') MYT_TGGLELO="${TRUE}";;
        'v') VERBOSE="${TRUE}";;
        'V') VERYVERB="${TRUE}";;
        'D') find_dot_file_zbksh -f "${MYT_PROGRAM}" -a "document" && return
4;;
        'E') find_dot_file_zbksh -f "${MYT_PROGRAM}" -a "example"  && return
5;;
        '?') find_dot_file_zbksh -f "${MYT_PROGRAM}" -a "usagemsg" && return
1 ;;
        ':') find_dot_file_zbksh -f "${MYT_PROGRAM}" -a "usagemsg" && return
2 ;;
        '#') find_dot_file_zbksh -f "${MYT_PROGRAM}" -a "usagemsg" && return
3 ;;
    esac
done

shift $(( ${OPTIND} - 1 ))

##################################################
```

If the "usagemsg" action is called from the "find_dot_file_zbksh"
function, the list of directories identified in the FPATH variable are
searched for the occurrence of a hidden file named
".my_template04_zbksh.usagemsg". This file is located in the same
directory with the "my_template04_zbksh" function and has the
following contents:

```
Program: my_template04_zbksh          Version: 1.0

Place a brief description ( < 255 chars ) of your shell
function here.

Usage: my_template04_zbksh [-?vV] [-u] [-l]

    Where:
        -u = Convert command line arguments to upper case
        -l = Convert command line arguments to lower case
        -D = Generate Documentation
        -E = Execute Examples in Usagemsg
        -v = Verbose mode - displays function info
        -V = Very Verbose Mode - debug output displayed
        -? = Help - display this message

Example Usage:
        my_template04_zbksh -v -u
        my_template04_zbksh -v -l

Author: Your Name (YourEmail@address.com)

\"AutoContent\" enabled
\"Multi-Shell\" enabled
```

The contents of the "usagemsg" file is read and displayed on STDERR.
This "usagemsg" file is simply a text file and may contain any information
desired and formatted to fit the requirements of any style guide.

The reader will notice there are a couple of additional command line options now defined as standard options; they are:

- D : Generate Documentation

- E : Execute Examples

These options are used to automatically generate documentation and it is recommended these options be included as standard options with all functions based on the Advanced Template. The list of recommended options to be included with all Advanced Shell Script functions is now:

- v : Verbose mode

- V : Very Verbose Mode

- D : Generate Documentation

- E : Execute Examples

- ? : Display Usage Message

- : : Missing Command Line Argument

- # : Missing Numeric Command Line Argument

The "D" and "E" command line options will be discussed in greater detail in the next chapter titled "Automated Documentation".

The reader will also notice the "my_template04_zbksh" file contains the function as well as the standalone portions of the script.

> *The above may be a desirable code configuration when writing new scripts.*

Obviously we have not completely explored or fully utilized the concept of a "function library" as of yet. So it will be examined further until all functions are externalized and referenced from the function library, and the standalone portion of the shell script is as small and simple as possible.

Before we expand the function library to the next step, it is desirable to include the concept of automated documentation into the discussion. This will permit the script programmer to automatically generate documentation for any script they write, and simplifies the administration processes for business continuity and data center automation.

The Business Continuity and Data Center Automation concepts enabled in the Advanced Template include the following:

Business Continuity Foundations

- Shell Script Programming Policies
    - o Reusable tasks written as functions
    - o Embedded documentation
    - o Function Libraries
    - o Usage Message Documentation
    - o Example Usage Code
- Shell Scripting Guidelines
    - o Multi-Shell Execution
    - o Usage message
    - o Dynamic configuration
    - o Command line option processing using "getopts"
    - o Unique Variable Naming
- Shell Scripting Standards
    - o Grutatxt markup for embedded comments
    - o Standardized Command Line Options
        - ▪ v : Verbose mode
        - ▪ V : Very Verbose Mode
        - ▪ D : Generate Documentation
        - ▪ E : Execute Examples
        - ▪ ? : Display Usage Message
        - ▪ : : Missing Command Line Argument
        - ▪ # : Missing Numeric Command Line Argument

- o   Example Code Execution
- Shell Scripting Procedures
  - o   ksh93 Function
  - o   Traps
  - o   Variable typesets
  - o   Local variables in functions
  - o   Embedded status reporting

The next chapter provides a detailed discussion of automated documentation and provides utilities for generating and managing that documentation.

_____

Chapter 7: Automated Documentation

One of the requirements for achieving Business Continuity is current up-to-date documentation for all critical processes and procedures. This is useful for numerous departments and scenarios such as:

- Support

- Maintenance

- Administration

- Cross-Training

- Onboarding new personnel

- Disaster Recovery

- And of course Data Center Automation

Before a procedure can be automated, it must be identified fully and completely. Each and every step, every command, and every possible deviation of results must be known. This level of information is obtained thru detailed scripting and documentation. The scripts and documentation must be available for peer review to ensure all components in the logic flow have been properly identified and accounted for.

Typically, system administrators enjoy creating automation scripts, but detest creating documentation. The solution to this incongruity is to convert the task of writing documentation into a scripting task. This chapter will describe a technique for embedding comments into the scripts, and then use these embedded comments to automatically generate documentation. This chapter will also provide an automated mechanism for uploading this generated documentation to a centralized location such as a MediaWiki Server.

To ensure that documentation is always up-to-date and current, the system administrator can schedule batch jobs to automatically generate documentation on a periodic basis, such as daily, weekly, monthly, etc. Once generated, the documentation can be automatically uploaded to the centralized documentation server. This technique eliminates the need for the script programmer to write documentation separately from the writing the shell script. The documentation becomes an embedded automation task thus reducing the workload of the system administrator and contributing to the Business Continuity environment.

This level of automation requires strict adherence to a shell script programming style guide.

In order to make the documentation task as simple as possible for the script programmer, this technique does not impose any formatting structures on the script programmer. The only requirement is the documentation be embedded into each script or function using a comment identifier that can be easily extracted. And there are several types of documentation that can be created by the script programmer. These documentation types include:

- Usage Message

    o .<*functionname*>_zbksh.conf

- Embedded Predefined Topics Section

    o Description - Place a full text description of your shell function here.

    o Assumptions - Provide a list of assumptions your shell function makes, with a description of each assumption.

    o Dependencies - Provide a list of dependencies your shell function has, with a description of each dependency.

    o Products - Provide a list of output your shell function produces, with a description of each product.

    o Configured Usage - Describe how your shell function should be used.

- Embedded Comments

- Example Output

The first documentation method identified above as the "Usage Message" requires the script programmer to create a text file containing instructions on how to use the function or script. This text file can be formatted to fit any documentation style guide, and is shown in this book using a "man" page style formatting. The file name of the usage message corresponds to the function name, however it must begin with a dot "." and end with a ".conf" suffix. The function "find_dot_file_zbksh" can be used within any other function to display the usage message, as has been seen previously in the "my_template04_zbksh" function. The usage message file associated with the "my_template04_zbksh" function is named ".my_template04_zbksh.conf" and is a hidden file.

To implement the Automated Documentation technique, a programming policy should be enforced so that every shell script function or script must have a corresponding "usagemsg" hidden file.

The second documentation method requires the script programmer to include a standardized set of documentation topics in each function or script. A suggested set of topics include:

- Description

- Assumptions

- Dependencies

- Products

- Configured Usage

- Details

This is simply a guideline for the documentation topics and should be modified to fit the organizations needs and requirements. Several examples of each topic are provided in the adv_zbksh function library.

Notice the leader string "#### " associated with each embedded comment in the following predefined topic section. The embedded comment leader string starts at the beginning of the line, followed by four (4) hash (#) marks, followed by a space character. This is the default definition of this leader string as utilized by the automated documentation technique described in this book. It can be changed to be anything the script programmer wants, but it will be shown and identified in this book as the regular expression"^#### ", meaning beginning of line, followed by four (4) hash (#) marks, followed by a single space.

```
####################################################
####
#### Description:
####
#### Place a full text description of your shell function here.
####
#### Assumptions:
####
#### Provide a list of assumptions your shell function makes,
#### with a description of each assumption.
####
#### Dependencies:
####
#### Provide a list of dependencies your shell function has,
#### with a description of each dependency.
####
#### Products:
####
#### Provide a list of output your shell function produces,
#### with a description of each product.
####
#### Configured Usage:
####
#### Describe how your shell function should be used.
####
#### Details:
####
#### Place nothing here, the details are your shell function.
####
####################################################
```

Notice that lines exist in the above example that do not contain any text other than the leader string. When extracted for the documentation, these will appear as blank lines.

The third type of documentation is free-form embedded comments scattered throughout the script or function. These comments provide a description of each command or section of code being executed. These comments can contain anything the script programmer thinks is relevant to understanding the code and processing being performed. These embedded comments also begin with the same leader string and are extracted using the "document" action of the find_dot_file_zbksh script. Alternatively these embedded scripts can be extracted using a simple grep command such as:

```
grep '^#### ' functionname_zbksh | sed -e 's/^#### //g'
```

The output from the "grep" command can be piped into a "sed" command to remove the leader string as shown above.

Some example embedded comments can be seen in the "my_template04_zbksh" such as:

```
#### Process the command line options and arguments.
```

```
#### Place any command line option error checking statements
#### here.  If an error is detected, print a message to
#### standard error, and return from this function with a
#### non-zero return code.

#### Your shell function should perform its specific work here.
#### All work performed by your shell function should be coded
#### within this section of the function.  This does not mean that
#### your function should be called from here, it means the shell
#### code that performs the work of your function should be
#### incorporated into the body of this function.  This should
#### become your function.

#### Main Body of Script Begins Here

#### Identify the function library directories to search
#### in the FPATH environment variable

#### Define the values for TRUE and FALSE,
#### In shell think, TRUE is zero (0) and FALSE is non-zero.

#### Extract the "shebang" line from the beginning of the script

#### Test the "shebang" line to determine what shell interpreter is
specified

#### Modify the shell specific commands and script according to the shell
interpreter
#### For those shell interpreters that do not directly support function
libraries,
#### cache all the *_zbksh functions found in the FPATH directories.

#### Loop thru each directory in the FPATH list using a colon (:)
delimeter.
#### Process each directory in reverse order to simulate results of
#### searching the FPATH directory.

#### Gather a list of functions ending in *_zbksh from the directory and
loop
#### thru each file using a â€œforâ€  loop.

#### Check each *_zbksh file to see if it starts with a function, if so
#### cache it in the current environment by running it as as a "dot"
script.

#### Call the script function to begin processing
```

Another feature of the function "find_dot_file_zbksh" is the ability to
execute the examples listed in the usage message, assuming the commands
adhere to a simple formatting standard. For example view the usage
message file ".my_template04_zbksh.usagemsg" and observe the
"Example Usage:" section of that document.

```
Example Usage:
    my_template04_zbksh -v -u
    my_template04_zbksh -v -l
```

Shown here are a couple of example command using the
"my_template04_zbksh" function. Notice the formatting of this section
begins with the literal header "Example Usage:", immediately followed by
one or more example commands, followed by one or more blank lines. If

the function "find_dot_file_zbksh" is executed with the "example" action command line option, the example commands will be executed and the results captured.

All four types of documentation can be automatically generated for the "my_template04_zbksh" function using the following standalone script:

```
#!/usr/bin/ksh93
#!/bin/bash
#################################################

FPATH="."
export FPATH

echo "#################################################"
my_template04_zbksh -D > .my_template04_zbksh.document 2>&1
my_template04_zbksh -E > .my_template04_zbksh.example  2>&1
```

The above script assumes it is being executed from the directory containing the shell script functions, and will create documentation files in that same directory.

Notice it is using the "-D" command line option to generate the documentation file, which will contain the usage message, embedded comments, and the output from executing the example commands.

The "-E" command line option causes the examples identified in the usage message file to be executed. The results are then captured in a file with the suffix ".example".

To generate the documentation for all functions in the Advanced Function Library which support the "-D" and/or "-E" command line options, a simple standalone script can be used as shown here:

```
#!/usr/bin/ksh93
#!/bin/bash
#################################################
FPATH="."
export FPATH

for F in $( grep -l -- "D.*find_dot_file_zbksh.*document" *_zbksh )
do
     echo ${F}
     ${F} -D > ${F}.document 2>&1
done

for F in $( grep -l -- "E.*find_dot_file_zbksh.*example" *_zbksh )
do
     echo ${F}
     ${F} -E > ${F}.example  2>&1
done
```

The above script assumes it is being executed from the directory containing the Advanced Function Library files. It searches the current directory for all files ending with "_zbksh" and lines containing the "find_dot_file_zbksh" command with the "document" or "example" actions.

It is recommended that each new standardized function created by a function programmer include the "-D" and "-E" options to automatically generate the function documentation. This means the function programmer must also create the Usage Message file, and embed comments in the function to be extracted as documentation.

Each function in the Advanced Function Library has the ability to generate its own documentation and execute its own examples. Once the documentation is generated, it should to be uploaded to a centralized documentation server, which can be accomplished in a number of different ways. There are a wide variety of file transfer mechanisms such as ftp, sftp, scp, nfs, etc.

Or we can use the MediaWiki server, however to automate this process requires some complex scripting. It also requires the API interface and "upload" functions to be enabled within the MediaWiki software. Administration of the MediaWiki server is outside the scope of this book and will be left to the reader to discover and perform. The Automated Documentation upload procedures described in this book will assume the MediaWiki server has been configured to allow file uploads using the API interface.

So the next step is to access the MediaWiki Server API interface and upload the documentation files. This is a complex procedure and requires multiple steps:

- Step 1 – Retrieve a login token from the MediaWiki Server

- Step 2 - Create a login session on the MediaWiki Server

- Step 3 - Retrieve an "editToken" from the MediaWiki Server

- Step 4 - Upload the page contents to the MediaWiki Server

Fortunately there is already a shell script function in the Advanced Function library to upload files to a MediaWiki Server. The function name is "wikiAutoLoad_zbksh" and the full source code of this function is contained in Appendix F. This script has numerous options which will be discussed here. These options include:

```
Function: wikiAutoLoad_zbksh      Version: 2.0

Multi-Shell Functions - Sort Function

Automatically upload files as page content to a Wiki Server.

    Usage: wikiAutoLoad_zbksh [-?vVfzxDE] [-u WikiUserName] [-p
WikiUserPassword]
                    [-a URL] [-t PageTitle] [-c CookieDir] [-o OutputDir]
                    [-C Category:...] [-e FileExension:...]
                    FileNamesToUpload...
    where:
        -u = WikiUser Login name (Default: WikiSysop)
        -p = WikiUser Password (Default: administrator)
        -a = Wiki API URL (Default: http://127.0.0.1/wiki/api.php )
        -t = Page Title (only valid for single file upload) (Default: NULL)
        -c = Directory for storage of HTTP cookies (Default: .)
        -o = Directory for storage of output files (Default: .)
        -C = WikiCategories to assign to each uploaded page (Default: Upload)
        -z = Preview Mode, show steps but do not upload anything (Default:
FALSE)
        -e = Delete matching file extension from upload files
             use remaining FileName suffix as the PageTitle
        -f = Insert Preformatted tags around file content (Default: FALSE)
        -x = Convert imbedded HTTP control characters to URL hex codes
        -D = Generate Documentation
        -E = Execute Examples in Usagemsg
        -v = Verbose mode - displays wikiAutoLoad function info
        -V = Very Verbose Mode - debug output displayed
        -? = Help - display this message

    Example: wikiAutoLoad -a "http://127.0.0.1/wiki/api.php" -p wikiuser -C
"Category" *.html

    Configuration File: ~/.wikiAutoLoad_zbksh.conf
    Usage Message File: ~/.wikiAutoLoad_zbksh.usagemsg

    Author: Dana French, Copyright 2016, All Rights Reserved

    "AutoContent" enabled (Grutatxt)
    "Multi-Shell" enabled
    "LocalRemote" enabled
```

As seen in previous scripts, all options have default values associated with them and several options are required. The required values are:

- Wiki User Login Name

  - Shell Variable: WAL_WIKIUSER

- Wiki User Password

  - Shell Variable: WAL_WIKIPASS

- Wiki API URL

  ○ Shell Variable: WAL_APIURL

- Upload File Name

It is recommended the script programmer should download the function "wikiAutoLoad_zbksh" to a local function library, then edit the values for the above variables to reflect the local requirements. See the shell variable initialization section for the default values.

Or the script programmer may want to create a configuration file named ".wikiAutoLoad_zbksh.conf" containing the following variable settings:

```
##################################################
####
#### This is the configuration file for the program "wikiAutoLoad_zbksh".
The
#### values show below are the default values for each configurable
variable.
#### If you want to change a value, copy the configuration line, uncomment
#### it, and change the value.
####
##################################################

# PROGRAM="wikiAutoLoad_zbksh"
# VERSION="2.0"
# WAL_WIKIUSER="wikiSysop"
# WAL_WIKIPASS="abcd1234"
# WAL_APIURL="http://127.0.0.1/wiki/api.php"
# WAL_PAGETITLE=""
# WAL_CATEGORIES="Upload"
```

In either case, whether the script programmer chooses to edit the function itself or create the configuration file, no command line arguments are required, and the documentation files can be uploaded to the MediaWiki Server with a very simple script such as:

```
#!/usr/bin/ksh93
#!/bin/bash
##################################################

FPATH="."
export FPATH

for i in .*.document
do
  wikiAutoLoad_zbksh -v "${i}"
done
```

The above script assumes it is being executed from the function library directory. It searches for all hidden files with a ".document" suffix and calls the function "wikiAutoLoad_zbksh" to upload each file.

Additional command line options can be provided such as the Page Title and Category. The default page title is the file name of the content being uploaded. The default category is "upload".

Another recommendation regarding embedded comments is to use "Grutatxt" formatting. This is a text markup style that can be easily converted between varieties of formats including HTML. This allows the script programmer to use a single formatting style to support numerous documentation requirements.

The Grutatxt Perl module can be downloaded from the Internet. There is also an Advanced Shell Function called "txt2html_zbksh" which will convert Grutatxt formatted text to HTML. This function may also be downloaded from the Internet and will be discussed in a future book of this series.

This concept of automated documentation is not limited to shell scripts. It can be easily implemented across a wide variety of script and compiled languages. It simply requires an enterprise wide mentality of Business Continuity and Data Center Automation.

Chapter 8: The Advanced Shell Script

If you have made it this far, congratulations! It has been a long road to get to this point, but this chapter is the payoff.

Here will be discussed externalizing all functions to the Function Library, and minimizing the standalone portions of a script using a standardized/customized "dot" file. To begin this discussion, review the various components of the Advanced Function Template:

- Multi-Shell Interpreter Shebang Line
- Korn Shell or POSIX Style Function declaration
  - Local variables can exist in Korn Shell Functions
  - Global variables in POSIX Functions
- Variable Initialization
- Dynamic Configuration File
- Command Line Option processing
- Command Line Argument Verification
- Display Function Configuration
- Command Processing specific to Functions
- External Usage Message File
- External Configuration File
- External Standalone Script

The one topic from the above list that we have not discussed thoroughly is the External Standalone Script. This is a very important part of the Advanced Function Library. It contains the Global variables needed by various functions in the library such as:

- FPATH

- ○ List of Library Directories

- SHCODE
  - ○ Shell Script Interpreter Identification

- GBL_ECHO
  - ○ Shell specific command to display output

When writing Advanced functions, the function programmer will initialize any global variables required by their functions in the standalone script before any library functions are called. The standalone script is a custom written script which is specific to each need or requirement. This script may call one (1) or more functions from one (1) or more function libraries. The point is the standalone shell script contains some standard definitions that will be needed in all scripts that call and reference functions from an Advanced Function Library.

Appendix G contains a full listing of all of the scripts, functions, and files that will be discussed in this chapter.

First, let's take a look at the standalone script named "my_template05.sh". Most of the components of this standalone script were discussed previously in Chapter 3, however there are additional components that need to be examined further.

The standalone shell script "my_template05.sh" begins with the expected list of "shebang" lines identifying the location of supported shell interpreters:

```
#!/usr/bin/ksh93
#!/bin/bash
#!/bin/zsh
####################################################
```

This is followed by the initialization of the FPATH environment variable. The FPATH variable contains a list of directories containing advanced shell script functions and will be used here by all shell interpreters, regardless of whether or not they natively support Function Libraries:

```
####
#### Identify the function library directories to search
#### in the FPATH environment variable
```

```
FPATH=~/functions/adv_zbksh:~/functions:/usr/local/functions
export FPATH
```

Any additional global variables are initialized next, including the values of
TRUE and FALSE. These variables are used by the Advanced Functions
to test numerous conditions and must be defined in the standalone shell
script:

```
####
#### Define the values for TRUE and FALSE,
#### In shell think, TRUE is zero (0) and FALSE is non-zero.

TRUE="0"
FALSE="1"
```

The dynamic determination of the shell script interpreter is performed
next. The first line of the current standalone shell script is retrieved and
stored in a shell variable named SHEBANG. This variable is used to
determine how the shell script programmer wants the script to be
interpreted:

```
####
#### Extract the "shebang" line from the beginning of the script

read SHEBANG < "${0}"
export SHEBANG
```

The SHEBANG shell variable is tested to determine if it contains specific
character strings. These strings correspond to various shell interpreters. If
the SHEBANG line contains the string "/ksh", the shell variable
SHCODE is set to the value "korn" and causes the remaining portion of
the script and all called functions to be interpreted as Korn Shell scripts.

If the SHEBANG line contains the string "/bash", the shell variable
SHCODE is set to the value "bash" and causes the remaining portion of
the script and all called functions to be interpreted as Bash scripts.

If the SHEBANG line contains the string "/zsh", the shell variable
SHCODE is set to the value "zshell" and causes the remaining portion of
the script and all called functions to be interpreted as Z-Shell scripts.

```
####
#### Test the "shebang" line to determine what shell interpreter is
specified

SHCODE="unknown"
[[ "_${SHEBANG}" == _*/ksh*  ]] && SHCODE="korn"
[[ "_${SHEBANG}" == _*/bash* ]] && SHCODE="bash"
[[ "_${SHEBANG}" == _*/zsh*  ]] && SHCODE="zshell"
export SHCODE
```

Any "shell specific" commands such as the "print" command in Korn shell are variablized in the next section. The Library functions should only reference the shell variable associated with these commands, and never use the shell specific command itself. In this way the commands can be dynamically modified according the shell interpreter being used. Also any shell options needed can be turned on or off in this section. As seen in the code below the shell option "extglob" turns on extended globbing in Bash. This enables Korn Shell-like variable options and substitutions and is needed to standardize the shell code across multiple shell interpreters:

```
####
#### Modify the shell specific commands and script according to the shell
interpreter

GBL_ECHO="echo -e"
[[ "_${SHCODE}" == "_korn"   ]] && GBL_ECHO="print --"
[[ "_${SHCODE}" == "_zshell" ]] && GBL_ECHO="print --" && emulate ksh93
[[ "_${SHCODE}" == "_bash"   ]] && shopt -s extglob    # Turn on extended
globbing
```

Since not all shells support the concept of "Shell Function Libraries", a workaround is included in the standalone shell script. This workaround caches all shell functions found in the directories specified by the FPATH variable. The normal behavior when searching the directories for a function is to use the first occurrence found of a function. However, since the workaround caches ALL functions found in the directories, if the workaround processes the directories in the order listed in the FPATH variable, this will have the effect of caching the LAST occurrence of each function.

To fix this potential issue in shell interpreters that do NOT natively support shell function libraries, the directories of the FPATH variable should be processed in REVERSE order listed. This will cause the last occurrence of a function to be in the first directory listed, and thus the expected behavior will be retained.

Since Korn Shell recognizes and uses the FPATH variable, it does not need to use the code below and is excluded from the test condition. Also the code below only searches for Advanced Functions ending with the "_zbksh" suffix:

```
####
#### For those shell interpreters that do not directly support function
libraries,
    #### cache all the *_zbksh functions found in the FPATH directories.
```

```
####
if [[ "_${SHCODE}" == "_zshell" ]] ||
   [[ "_${SHCODE}" == "_bash"   ]]
then

    #### Loop thru each directory in the FPATH list using a colon (:)
delimeter.
    #### Process each directory in reverse order to simulate results of
    #### searching the FPATH directory.

        IFS=":"
        FDIRS=( ${FPATH} )
        IFS=$' \t\n'

        END=${#FDIRS[@]}
        for (( IDX=END-1; IDX>=0; --IDX ))
        do
            FDIR="${FDIRS[${IDX}]}"

    #### Gather a list of functions ending in *_zbksh from the directory and
loop
    #### thru each file using a â€œforâ€ loop.

            for FUNC in ${FDIR}/*_zbksh
            do
    ####
    #### Check each *_zbksh file to see if it starts with a function, if so
    #### cache it in the current environment by running it as as a "dot"
script.
    ####
                if head -1 "${FUNC}" 2>/dev/null | egrep 'function|\(\)' >
/dev/null 2>&1
                then
                    . "${FUNC}"
                fi
            done
        done

        IFS=$' \t\n'

fi
```

The standalone script, regardless of shell interpreter, is now prepared to call a function from the Advanced Function Library. One or more functions can be called and any new shell code may be included beyond this point. In this example, the function named "my_template05_zbksh" is called and all command line arguments are passed to it using the shell variable "${@}":

```
####
#### Call the script function to begin processing
my_template05_zbksh "${@}"
```

Now let's run a few tests to prove this works with all functions now externalized and being called from the Advanced Function Library. In this first script execution, run the script as a "ksh93" script. Edit the script and specify the full path file name of the Korn Shell 93 interpreter as the SHEBANG line:

```
#!/usr/bin/ksh93
#!/bin/bash
#!/bin/zsh
##################################################
```

Then run the script:

```
$ ./my_template05.sh
Hello World!
```

In previous tests we saw that if no command line arguments were specified, then nothing was displayed. However, here we see it display "Hello World!" This is because a configuration file already exists for the function and is named ".my_template05_zbksh.conf". The contents of this configuration file are:

```
$ cat .my_template05_zbksh.conf
##################################################
####
#### This is the configuration file for the program "my_template05_zbksh".
The
#### values show below are the default values for each configurable
variable.
#### If you want to change a value, copy the configuration line, uncomment
#### it, and change the value.
####
##################################################

# MYT_PROGRAM="my_template05_zbksh"

# VERSION="1.0"

MYT_MSG="Hello World!"
```

Run it again with the "-?" command line argument to cause it to display the usage message:

```
$ ./my_template05.sh -?

Program: my_template05_zbksh          Version: 1.0

Place a brief description ( < 255 chars ) of your shell
function here.

Usage: my_template05_zbksh [-?vV] [-u] [-l]

    where:
       -u = Convert command line arguments to upper case
       -l = Convert command line arguments to lower case
       -D = Generate Documentation
       -E = Execute Examples in Usagemsg
       -v = Verbose mode - displays function info
       -V = Very Verbose Mode - debug output displayed
       -? = Help - display this message

    Example Usage:
```

```
my_template05_zbksh -v -u
my_template05_zbksh -v -l

Author: Your Name (YourEmail@address.com)

"AutoContent" enabled
"Multi-Shell" enabled
```

Now run the script using the upper case conversion option, then the lower case conversion option, then both options at the same time.

```
$ ./my_template05.sh -u
HELLO WORLD!

$ ./my_template05.sh -l
hello world!

$ ./my_template05.sh -u -l
# ERROR: Do not specify both upper and lower case conversion together

Program: my_template05_zbksh          Version: 1.0

Place a brief description ( < 255 chars ) of your shell
function here.

Usage: my_template05_zbksh [-?vV] [-u] [-l]

  Where:
    -u = Convert command line arguments to upper case
    -l = Convert command line arguments to lower case
    -D = Generate Documentation
    -E = Execute Examples in Usagemsg
    -v = Verbose mode - displays function info
    -V = Very Verbose Mode - debug output displayed
    -? = Help - display this message

Example Usage:
    my_template05_zbksh -v -u
    my_template05_zbksh -v -l

Author: Your Name (YourEmail@address.com)

"AutoContent" enabled
"Multi-Shell" enabled
```

Now change the SHEBANG line to bash, and re-run the script commands. The results should be the same.

```
vi my_template05.sh
#!/usr/bin/ksh93
#!/bin/bash
#!/bin/zsh
################################################
####
#### This script will run in KornShell93, Zshell, or Bash, all you need to
do
#### is put the desired "shebang" line at the top of the script.
####
################################################
...
...
...
:wq
```

```
$ ./my_template05.sh -u
HELLO WORLD!

$ ./my_template05.sh -l
hello world!

$ ./my_template05.sh -u -l
# ERROR: Do not specify both upper and lower case conversion together

Program: my_template05_zbksh        Version: 1.0

Place a brief description ( < 255 chars ) of your shell
function here.

Usage: my_template05_zbksh [-?vV] [-u] [-l]

    where:
      -u = Convert command line arguments to upper case
      -l = Convert command line arguments to lower case
      -D = Generate Documentation
      -E = Execute Examples in Usagemsg
      -v = Verbose mode - displays function info
      -V = Very Verbose Mode - debug output displayed
      -? = Help - display this message

Example Usage:
      my_template05_zbksh -v -u
      my_template05_zbksh -v -l

Author: Your Name (YourEmail@address.com)

"AutoContent" enabled
"Multi-Shell" enabled
```

Re-run the script as many times as you want, changing the SHEBANG line for each new shell interpreter you want to test. Use the "-v" and "-V" options to display the VERBOSE and VERYVERB output.

The Advanced Shell Script should perform **exactly** the same as you have seen previously. The difference now is that all functions are externalized and being referenced from the Advanced Function Library.

Even though all functions are now externalized, the thought of having to include the Function Library initialization code in every standalone script is not appealing. Therefore, add one more level of externalizing code. Externalize the Function Library initialization code into a centralized "dot" script and then include that "dot" script in each standalone scripts that references the Advanced Function Library. This will significantly reduce the required code for each standalone script and simplify it at the same time.

Review the standalone shell script named "adv_template05.sh":

```
$ cat adv_template05.sh
#!/usr/bin/ksh93
#!/bin/bash
#!/bin/zsh
##################################################
```

```
####
#### Extract the "shebang" line from the beginning of the script

read SHEBANG < "${0}"
export SHEBANG

####
#### Identify the function library directories to search
#### in the FPATH environment variable

FPATH=~/functions/adv_zbksh:~/functions:/usr/local/functions
export FPATH

if   [[ -f ./.adv_zbksh.prefix ]]
then     . ./.adv_zbksh.prefix
elif [[ -f ~/.adv_zbksh.prefix ]]
then     . ~/.adv_zbksh.prefix
fi

####
#### Call the script function to begin processing

my_template05_zbksh "${@}"
```

You should recognize a significant difference between "adv_template05.sh" and the previous iteration of the same script named "my_template05.sh". The "adv-template05.sh" version of the standalone shell script is greatly reduced by moving the Function Library initialization code into a centralized "dot" script named ".adv_zbksh.prefix". Here the "dot" script is located in the current directory or in the users' home directory. The content of the "dot" script contains:

```
####
#### Define the values for TRUE and FALSE,
#### In shell think, TRUE is zero (0) and FALSE is non-zero.

TRUE="0"
FALSE="1"

# ####
# #### Extract the "shebang" line from the beginning of the script
#
# read SHEBANG < "${0}"
# export SHEBANG
#
####
#### Test the "shebang" line to determine what shell interpreter is
specified

SHCODE="unknown"
[[ "_${SHEBANG}" == _*/ksh*  ]] && SHCODE="korn"
[[ "_${SHEBANG}" == _*/bash* ]] && SHCODE="bash"
[[ "_${SHEBANG}" == _*/zsh*  ]] && SHCODE="zshell"
export SHCODE

####
#### Modify the shell specific commands and script according to the shell
interpreter

GBL_ECHO="echo -e"
[[ "_${SHCODE}" == "_korn"   ]] && GBL_ECHO="print --"
[[ "_${SHCODE}" == "_zshell" ]] && GBL_ECHO="print --" && emulate ksh93
```

```
    [[ "_${SHCODE}" == "_bash"   ]] && shopt -s extglob    # Turn on extended
globbing

    ####
    #### For those shell interpreters that do not directly support function
libraries,
    #### cache all the *_zbksh functions found in the FPATH directories.
    ####

    if [[ "_${SHCODE}" == "_zshell" ]] ||
       [[ "_${SHCODE}" == "_bash"   ]]
    then

    #### Loop thru each directory in the FPATH list using a colon (:)
delimiter.
    #### Process each directory in reverse order to simulate results of
    #### searching the FPATH directory.

        IFS=":"
        FDIRS=( ${FPATH} )
        IFS=$' \t\n'

        END=${#FDIRS[@]}
        for (( IDX=END-1; IDX>=0; --IDX ))
        do
            FDIR="${FDIRS[${IDX}]}"

    #### Gather a list of functions ending in *_zbksh from the directory and
loop
    #### thru each file using a â€œforâ€ loop.

            for FUNC in ${FDIR}/*_zbksh
            do
    ####
    #### Check each *_zbksh file to see if it starts with a function, if so
    #### cache it in the current environment by running it as as a "dot"
script.
    ####
                if head -1 "${FUNC}" 2>/dev/null | egrep 'function|\(\)' >
/dev/null 2>&1
                then
                    . "${FUNC}"
                fi
            done
        done

        IFS=$' \t\n'

    fi
```

By externalizing the Function Library initialization code into a centralized
"dot" script, it allows the script programmer to focus their attention on
the functions they are writing rather than managing the function library(s).
The Function Library initialization "dot" script can be a single script for
all users on the system, or individualized by user as shown here. In this
way each script programmer or user may select the Function Libraries
needed to provide the desired functions. Or a centralized "dot" script may
be specified to standardize all Shell Scripts.

Now execute the tests again using the Advanced Shell Script with all functions externalized and the function library initialization code externalized.

Then run the script:

```
$ ./adv_template05.sh
Hello World!
```

Recognize that when the "adv_template05.sh" script is executed, it is calling the same Library Function as the previous script "my_template05.sh". The Library Function called by both scripts is named "my_template05_zbksh". This function used the same configuration file ".my_template05.conf" in both instances. Therefore, the "Hello World!" value is displayed again:

```
$ cat .my_template05_zbksh.conf
##################################################
####
#### This is the configuration file for the program "my_template05_zbksh".
The
#### values show below are the default values for each configurable
variable.
#### If you want to change a value, copy the configuration line, uncomment
#### it, and change the value.
####
##################################################

# MYT_PROGRAM="my_template05_zbksh"

# VERSION="1.0"

MYT_MSG="Hello World!"
```

Verify the command line option "-?" displays the usage message as seen previously:

```
$ ./adv_template05.sh -?

Program: my_template05_zbksh          Version: 1.0

Place a brief description ( < 255 chars ) of your shell
function here.

Usage: my_template05_zbksh [-?vV] [-u] [-1]

   Where:
      -u = Convert command line arguments to upper case
      -1 = Convert command line arguments to lower case
      -D = Generate Documentation
      -E = Execute Examples in Usagemsg
      -v = Verbose mode - displays function info
      -V = Very Verbose Mode - debug output displayed
      -? = Help - display this message

Example Usage:
      my_template05_zbksh -v -u
      my_template05_zbksh -v -1
```

```
Author: Your Name (YourEmail@address.com)

"AutoContent" enabled
"Multi-Shell" enabled
```

Notice the usage message is for the Library Function "my_template05_zbksh" because this is the function called by the standalone shell script "adv_template05.sh". Verify the other command line options work the same as seen before:

```
$ ./adv_template05.sh -u
HELLO WORLD!

$ ./adv_template05.sh -l
hello world!

$ ./adv_template05.sh -u -l
# ERROR: Do not specify both upper and lower case conversion together

Program: my_template05_zbksh        Version: 1.0

Place a brief description ( < 255 chars ) of your shell
function here.

Usage: my_template05_zbksh [-?vV] [-u] [-l]

   where:
     -u = Convert command line arguments to upper case
     -l = Convert command line arguments to lower case
     -D = Generate Documentation
     -E = Execute Examples in Usagemsg
     -v = Verbose mode - displays function info
     -V = Very Verbose Mode - debug output displayed
     -? = Help - display this message

Example Usage:
     my_template05_zbksh -v -u
     my_template05_zbksh -v -l

Author: Your Name (YourEmail@address.com)

"AutoContent" enabled
"Multi-Shell" enabled
```

Now change the SHEBANG line to bash, and re-run the script commands. The results should be the same.

```
vi adv_template05.sh
#!/bin/bash
#!/usr/bin/ksh93
#!/bin/zsh
##################################################
####
#### This script will run in KornShell93, Zshell, or Bash, all you need to
do
#### is put the desired "shebang" line at the top of the script.
####
##################################################
  ...
  ...
  ...
:wq

$ ./adv_template05.sh -u
```

```
HELLO WORLD!

$ ./adv_template05.sh -l
hello world!

$ ./adv_template05.sh -u -l
# ERROR: Do not specify both upper and lower case conversion together

Program: my_template05_zbksh          Version: 1.0

Place a brief description ( < 255 chars ) of your shell
function here.

Usage: my_template05_zbksh [-?vV] [-u] [-l]

   where:
      -u = Convert command line arguments to upper case
      -l = Convert command line arguments to lower case
      -D = Generate Documentation
      -E = Execute Examples in Usagemsg
      -v = Verbose mode - displays function info
      -V = Very Verbose Mode - debug output displayed
      -? = Help - display this message

Example Usage:
      my_template05_zbksh -v -u
      my_template05_zbksh -v -l

Author: Your Name (YourEmail@address.com)

"AutoContent" enabled
"Multi-Shell" enabled
```

Re-run the script as many times as you want, changing the SHEBANG
line for each new shell interpreter you want to test. Use the "-v" and "-V"
options to display the VERBOSE and VERYVERB output.

Again, the Advanced Shell Script with the Function Library Initialization
code externalized should perform **exactly** the same as you have seen
previously.

At this point, the function and script programmers have an Advanced
Shell Script Template that can be used for any purpose and a variety of
shell script interpreters. There are several variations of this template that
may be implemented by the script programmer which include:

- Partially Externalized: Chapter 6

  Standalone script with embedded functions and Advanced Function
  Library

- Fully Externalized: Chapter 8

  Standalone script with all functions externalized in Advanced
  Function Library

- Fully Externalized with External Initialization: Chapter 8

  Standalone script with all functions externalized in Function Library and library initialization externalized

You may think we are finished, but you would be wrong. What else can we possibly add to this Advanced Function Template? The answer is: The capability of executing commands locally or remote, which is the topic of the next chapter.

Chapter 9: Local/ Remote Command Execution

Just one more Advanced Shell Script Programming concept to go! This is the concept of writing your functions so the commands within the function can be executed locally or remote, depending upon where the user decides they need to run. Many times, scripts are written then copied to multiple remote systems where they are executed. A more advanced technique is to automatically detect whether a command should be executed locally or remote, and then run the command on the selected system. This technique allows the scripts and function libraries to be centralized on a single script server and executed from a single location.

In the example discussed here , remote command execution is achieved using a password-less SSH command.

The Advanced Function Library includes a function named "execl_zbksh" and provides the script programmer with the capability to dynamically execute a command on the local system, or a remote system if password-less SSH keys have been exchanged. A command or list of commands is specified as a single command line argument to the function "execl_zbksh". An example of using the function is shown here:

```
execl_zbksh "hostname; date"
```

The example above causes the function execl_zbksh to execute the list of commands "hostname; date" on the local system. If the script programmer wanted to execute this same list of commands on a remote system as the user "sshuser", the function call would be:

```
execl_zbksh -u sshuser -a remotesys.domain.com "hostname; date"
```

The execution of commands on remote systems using password-less SSH requires security and encryption keys be exchanged between the system running the shell script and all systems where remote commands will be executed. This exchange of SSH Keys must be performed before attempting to execute remote commands and is outside the scope of this topic. If you need information about how to set up SSH keys for remote command execution, a quick Internet search will return ample documentation on the subject.

Full source code and documentation for the Advanced Function named "execl_zbksh" is available in Appendix H.

The Advanced Function "execl_zbksh" will be examined here. This function is written using the Advanced Function Template and contains all of the sections discussed thus far.

The usage message for the function "execl_zbksh" provides a short description and a list of the command line options:

```
Function: execl_zbksh    Version: 1.0

Multi-Shell Functions - Execute a command locally or remote

Usage: execl_zbksh [-?vV] [-p port] [-u username] [-a ipaddress]
"cmdstring"

  where:

    -p sshport   = SSH Port Number
    -u username  = SSH User Name
    -a ipaddress = Remote IP Address of SSH Target
    -v   = Verbose mode - displays function info
    -V   = Very Verbose Mode - debug output displayed

Example Usage:
    execl_zbksh "date; hostname"

Configuration File: ~/.execl_zbksh.conf
Usage Message File: ~/.execl_zbksh.usagemsg

Author: Dana French, Copyright 2016, All Rights Reserved

"AutoContent" enabled (Grutatxt)
"Multi-Shell" enabled
"LocalRemote" enabled
```

The function "execl_zbksh" starts with a "Korn Shell" style function declaration followed by variable initialization:

```
function execl_zbksh {
#### ##################################################

  typeset PROGRAM="execl_zbksh"
  typeset VERSION="1.0"
  typeset TRUE="0"
  typeset FALSE="1"
  typeset VERBOSE="${FALSE}"
  typeset VERYVERB="${FALSE}"
  typeset OPTIND="1"
  typeset OPT_SSH="-o UserKnownHostsFile=/dev/null -o
StrictHostKeyChecking=no -o LogLevel=quiet -o BatchMode=yes -o
ConnectTimeout=30"
  typeset CMD_SSH="ssh"
  typeset SSHPORT=22
  typeset SSHUSER="sshuser"
  typeset SSHADDR=""
  typeset RETCODE="99"
```

The variables of note include:

- OPT_SSH : Command line options to the SSH commands

- CMD_SSH : Full directory path to the SSH Command

- SSHPORT : Ethernet port to use for SSH communications with remote system

- SSHUSER : Username on remote system with password-less SSH access enabled

- SSHADDR : Hostname or IP address of remote system

The default values for each of these variables should be modified to fit the script programmer's needs and requirements. However the variable "SSHADDR" should normally be left blank or NULL. This is because the function "execl_zbksh" uses this variable to determine whether to execute a specified command locally or remotely. If the variable SSHADDR is null, the command is executed locally. If the value of SSHADDR is NOT NULL, the function attempts to execute the command on the remote system specified by the value of SSHADDR.

Additionally the above shell variables can be defined in the configuration file "execl_zbksh.conf". This file is included into the function by the command:

```
#####################################################
    find_dot_file_zbksh -f "execl_zbksh" -a "configure"
#####################################################
```

Command line option processing occurs normally as has been described in previous chapters. Notice the SSH variables can all be specified on the command line as well.

```
#####################################################
####
#### Process the command line options and arguments, saving
#### the values as appropriate.
####

    while getopts ":vVDEp:u:a:" OPTION
    do
        case "${OPTION}" in
            'p')  SSHPORT="${OPTARG}";;
            'u')  SSHUSER="${OPTARG}";;
            'a')  SSHADDR="${OPTARG}";;
```

```
          'v')  VERBOSE="${TRUE}";;
          'V')  VERYVERB="${TRUE}";;
          'D')  find_dot_file_zbksh -f "${PROGRAM}" -a "document" && return
4;;
          'E')  find_dot_file_zbksh -f "${PROGRAM}" -a "example" && return
5;;
          '?')  find_dot_file_zbksh -f "${PROGRAM}" -a "usagemsg" && return
1 ;;
          ':')  find_dot_file_zbksh -f "${PROGRAM}" -a "usagemsg" && return
2 ;;
          '#')  find_dot_file_zbksh -f "${PROGRAM}" -a "usagemsg" && return
3 ;;
        esac
    done

    shift $(( ${OPTIND} - 1 ))
    [[ "_${1}" == "_--" ]] && shift 1
    [[ "_${1}" == "_--" ]] && shift 1
    [[ "_${1}" == "_--" ]] && shift 1

    #################################################
```

The command line arguments are verified, and any problems cause the
function to display the usage message and return. One of the variable
conflict issues that may be encountered is a non-NULL value for
SSHADDR and a NULL value for the SSHPORT. If the SSH address is
specified then the SSH Port must also be specified. The same is true for
the SSH User. If the SSH address is specified, the SSH Port and User
must also have non-NULL values. These values may be specified on the
command line, variable initialization section of the "execl_zbksh"
function, or in the configuration file "execl_zbksh.conf".

```
    #################################################
    ####
    #### Check the command line arguments to verify they are valid values and
that all
    #### necessary information was specified.
    ####

    trap "find_dot_file_zbksh -f execl_zbksh -a usagemsg" EXIT

    if [[ "_${SSHADDR}" != "_-" ]] &&
       [[ "_${SSHPORT}" == "_-" ]]
    then
      stderr_zbksh -- "# ERROR: SSH Port not specified"
      return 10
    fi

    if [[ "_${SSHADDR}" != "_-" ]] &&
       [[ "_${SSHUSER}" == "_-" ]]
    then
      stderr_zbksh -- "# ERROR: SSH User not specified"
      return 11
    fi

    trap "-" EXIT

    #################################################
```

In order to dynamically determine whether the specified command should be executed locally or remote, the function uses a rarely used variable substitution operator ":+". The definition of this variable operator is to examine the value of the variable and if the value is unset or NULL, then use NULL as the value of the variable. If the value of the variable set or not NULL, do not use the current value, instead use the value specified after the variable operator. This variable operator is used to assign a value to the EXECMODE shell variable as follows:

```
EXECMODE="${SSHADDR:+${CMD_SSH} ${OPT_SSH} -p ${SSHPORT}
${SSHUSER}@${SSHADDR}}"
```

In regular English, the above command:

- Tests the value of the SHADDR variable to determine if it is unset or NULL.

  o If so, it assigns NULL to the EXECMODE shell variable.

  o If not, it substitutes the value following the operator to EXECMODE.

So if an IP address or a hostname was specified on the command line or in the configuration file, an SSH command line is built and assigned to the EXECMODE variable. This SSH command line is used to execute a command on a remote system.

In summary, if an IP Address or hostname is specified, the EXECMODE variable will be assigned an SSH command line. If no IP address or hostname is specified, the EXECMODE variable will be NULL.

```
#####################################################
####
#### Define the command execution mode, either local or remote depending
upon
#### the value of the SSHADDR variable. If it contains a remote IP address
or
#### hostname, define the execution mode variable. Otherwise it are set to
#### NULL, which means the commands will run locally.

    EXECMODE="${SSHADDR:+${CMD_SSH} ${OPT_SSH} -p ${SSHPORT}
${SSHUSER}@${SSHADDR}}"

    verbose_comment_zbksh -v "${VERBOSE}" -c "${EXECMODE:-eval} \"${@}\""

    ${EXECMODE:-eval} "${@}"
    RETCODE="${?}"

    return ${RETCODE}

}
####
```

```
#### ##################################################
```

The next variable operator to notice is ":-" and it is associated with the command:

```
${EXECMODE:-eval} "${@}"
```

In regular English, this variable operator tests the value of the variable EXECMODE to determine if it is unset or NULL. If so, it substitutes the value following the variable operator, which is "eval". If not (meaning the variable EXECMODE has a value), then it uses the value assigned to the variable.

So if EXECMODE is NULL, the value "eval" is substituted on the command line and followed by all command line arguments to the function, i.e., "${@}".

```
eval "hostname; date"
```

In the above example, the value of "${@}" is substituted with the value "hostname; date"

If EXECMODE is Not NULL, the value of EXECMODE is substituted on the command line and followed by all command line arguments to the function, i.e., "${@}":

```
ssh -o LogLevel=quiet -p 22 sshuser@remotesys.domain.com "hostname; date"
```

So depending upon the value of the SSHADDR shell variable, the specified commands are executed either locally or remotely. The return code of executing the commands is captured and assigned to the shell variable RETCODE, and this value is used as the return code from the function "execl_zbksh".

Using this function, "execl_zbksh", the function or script programmer can write functions that will perform actions across multiple systems, groups, or entire data centers, and collect the results on the originating system.

The next book in this series will focus precisely on this function, "execl_zbksh", and provide multiple automated mechanisms for configuration, software management, testing, monitoring, and support across multiple operating systems, shell environments, platforms, architectures, and data centers.

Chapter 10: Conclusion

The objective of this book has been to delineate the role that Advanced Shell Script Programming can play in today's automated and cloud based data center environments. As with other programming languages, there is a need for shell scripting code to be standardized and organized across all environments and data centers in an organization. The concepts presented here show how that can be done. To review the objectives of this book:

- Provide a standardized shell scripting template that can be used repeatedly and consistently to build function libraries.

- Identification of shell scripting components of Business Continuity.

- Implementation of Data Center Automation techniques for documentation, training, support, and maintenance.

- Standardization and Centralization of Code

The Advanced Function Template contains numerous components that provides the shell script programmer with the ability to write standardized code. These components include:

- Multi-Shell Interpreter Shebang Line

- Korn Shell or POSIX Style Function declaration

  - Local variables can exist in Korn Shell Functions

  - Global variables in POSIX Functions

- Variable Initialization

- Dynamic Configuration File

- Command Line Option processing

- Command Line Argument Verification

- Display Function Configuration

- Command Processing specific to Functions

- External Usage Message File

- External Configuration File

- External Standalone Script

The techniques and methodologies discussed in this book contribute to the overall mentality of Business Continuity. As a review, Business Continuity is an enterprise wide mentality of conducting day-to-day business. This mentality ensures the organization will be able to continue conducting business regardless of any adversities encountered. These adversities may include:

- Facility or Physical issues.

- Scheduled or unscheduled outages.

- Onboarding of new personnel

- Training of existing personnel

- Off-boarding of personnel

- Unexpected loss of personnel

- Support and Maintenance

- Auditing

- Documentation

By implementing the concepts described in this book, the reader will be able to provide their organization with the ability to control and integrate Data Center Automation (DCA) efforts directly into their Business Continuity plans as follows:

Business Continuity Foundations

- Shell Script Programming Policies

  - Reusable tasks written as functions

  - Embedded documentation

- ○ Function Libraries
- ○ Usage Message Documentation
- ○ Function Level Documentation
- ○ Example Usage Code
- Shell Scripting Guidelines
  - ○ Multi-Shell Execution
  - ○ Usage message
  - ○ Dynamic configuration
  - ○ Command line option processing using "getopts"
  - ○ Unique Variable Naming
- Shell Scripting Standards
  - ○ Grutatxt markup for embedded comments
  - ○ Standardized Command Line Options
    - ▪ v : Verbose mode
    - ▪ V : Very Verbose Mode
    - ▪ D : Generate Documentation
    - ▪ E : Execute Examples
    - ▪ ? : Display Usage Message
    - ▪ : : Missing Command Line Argument
    - ▪ # : Missing Numeric Command Line Argument
  - ○ Example Code Execution
- Shell Scripting Procedures
  - ○ ksh93 Function
  - ○ Traps

- ○ Variable typesets

- ○ Local variables in functions

- ○ Embedded status reporting

Now that a standardized shell script function template has been defined and thoroughly examined, it can be used to build and integrate Data Center Automation tasks. The next book in this series will discuss several techniques and methodologies to achieve Data Center Automation in the areas of deployment, verification, testing, and auditing.

Appendix A

Function: my_template01_k93

```
#!/usr/bin/ksh93
##################################################
function usagemsg_my_template01_k93 {
  print "
Program: my_template01_k93

Place a brief description ( < 255 chars ) of your shell
function here.

Usage: ${1##*/} [-?vV]

  Where:
    -v = Verbose mode - displays my_template01_k93 function info
    -V = Very Verbose Mode - debug output displayed
    -? = Help - display this message

Author: Your Name (YourEmail@address.com)
\"AutoContent\" enabled
"
}
##################################################
####
#### Description:
####
#### Place a full text description of your shell function here.
####
#### Assumptions:
####
#### Provide a list of assumptions your shell function makes,
#### with a description of each assumption.
####
#### Dependencies:
####
#### Provide a list of dependencies your shell function has,
#### with a description of each dependency.
####
#### Products:
####
#### Provide a list of output your shell function produces,
#### with a description of each product.
####
#### Configured Usage:
####
#### Describe how your shell function should be used.
####
#### Details:
####
#### Place nothing here, the details are your shell function.
####
##################################################
configure_my_template01_k93()
{
####
#### Notice this function is a POSIX function so that it can see local
#### and global variables from calling functions and scripts.
####
#### Configuration parameters can be stored in a file and
#### this script can be dynamically reconfigured by sending
#### the running script a HUP signal using the kill command.
####
#### Configuration variables can be defined in the configuration file using
#### the same syntax as defining a shell variable, e.g.: VARIABLE="value"
```

```
    CFILE=~/.my_template01_k93.conf

    (( VERBOSE == TRUE )) && print -- "# Configuration File: ${CFILE}"

    if [[ -f ${CFILE} ]]
    then
        (( VERBOSE == TRUE )) && cat ${CFILE}
        . ${CFILE}
    fi

    return 0
}
####################################################
function my_template01_k93 {
    typeset VERSION="1.0"
    typeset TRUE="0"
    typeset FALSE="1"
    typeset VERBOSE="${FALSE}"
    typeset VERYVERB="${FALSE}"

#### Set up a trap of the HUP signal to cause this script
#### to dynamically configure or reconfigure itself upon
#### receipt of the HUP signal.

    trap "configure_my_template01_k93 ${0}" HUP

#### Read the configuration file and initialize variables by
#### sending this script a HUP signal

    kill -HUP ${$}

#### Process the command line options and arguments.

    while getopts ":vV" OPTION
    do
        case "${OPTION}" in
            'v') VERBOSE="${TRUE}";;
            'V') VERYVERB="${TRUE}";;
            '?') usagemsg_my_template01_k93 "${0}" && return 1 ;;
            ':') usagemsg_my_template01_k93 "${0}" && return 2 ;;
            '#') usagemsg_my_template01_k93 "${0}" && return 3 ;;
        esac
    done

    shift $(( ${OPTIND} - 1 ))

    trap "usagemsg_my_template01_k93 ${0}" EXIT

#### Place any command line option error checking statements
#### here.  If an error is detected, print a message to
#### standard error, and return from this function with a
#### non-zero return code.  The "trap" statement will cause
#### the "usagemsg" to be displayed.

    trap "-" EXIT

    (( VERYVERB == TRUE )) && set -x
    (( VERBOSE  == TRUE )) && print -u 2 "# Version..........: ${VERSION}"

    MSG="${@}"

####################################################

####
#### Your shell function should perform it's specific work here.
#### All work performed by your shell function should be coded
#### within this section of the function.  This does not mean that
#### your function should be called from here, it means the shell
#### code that performs the work of your function should be
#### incorporated into the body of this function.  This should
#### become your function.
####
```

```
  (( VERBOSE  == TRUE )) && print -u 2 "# MSG Variable Value: ${MSG}"
  print -- "${MSG}"

  trap "-" HUP

  return 0
}
##################################################
my_template01_k93 "${@}"
```

Appendix B

Function: my_template02_zbksh

```
#!/usr/bin/ksh93
#!/bin/bash
#!/bin/zsh
##################################################
####
#### This script will run in KornShell93, Zshell, or Bash, all you need to do
#### is put the desired "shebang" line at the top of the script.
####
##################################################
function usagemsg_my_template02_zbksh {
  CMD_ECHO="${GBL_ECHO:-echo -e }"
  ${CMD_ECHO} ""
  ${CMD_ECHO} "${1:+Program: ${1}}${2:+         Version: ${2}}"

  ${CMD_ECHO} "
Place a brief description ( < 255 chars ) of your shell
function here.

Usage: ${1##*/} [-?vV] [-u] [-l]

   Where:
     -u = Convert command line arguments to upper case
     -l = Convert command line arguments to lower case
     -v = Verbose mode - displays my_template02_zbksh function info
     -V = Very Verbose Mode - debug output displayed
     -? = Help - display this message

Author: Your Name (YourEmail@address.com)

\"AutoContent\" enabled
\"Multi-Shell\" enabled
"
}
##################################################
####
#### Description:
####
#### Place a full text description of your shell function here.
####
#### Assumptions:
####
#### Provide a list of assumptions your shell function makes,
#### with a description of each assumption.
####
#### Dependencies:
####
#### Provide a list of dependencies your shell function has,
#### with a description of each dependency.
####
#### Products:
####
#### Provide a list of output your shell function produces,
#### with a description of each product.
####
#### Configured Usage:
####
#### Describe how your shell function should be used.
####
#### Details:
####
#### Place nothing here, the details are your shell function.
####
```

```
#################################################
configure_my_template02_zbksh()
{
####
#### Notice this function is a POSIX function so that it can see local
#### and global variables from calling functions and scripts.
####
#### Configuration parameters can be stored in a file and
#### this script can be dynamically reconfigured by sending
#### the running script a HUP signal using the kill command.
####
#### Configuration variables can be defined in the configuration file using
#### the same syntax as defining a shell variable, e.g.: VARIABLE="value"

    CMD_ECHO="${GBL_ECHO:-echo -e }"

    [[ "_${1}" != "_" ]] && MYT_CFILE=~/.${1}.conf

    (( VERBOSE == TRUE )) && ${CMD_ECHO} "# Configuration File: ${MYT_CFILE}"

    if [[ -f ${MYT_CFILE} ]]
    then
        (( VERBOSE == TRUE )) && cat ${MYT_CFILE}
        . ${MYT_CFILE}
    fi

    return 0
}
#################################################
function my_template02_zbksh {

    typeset TRUE="${TRUE:-0}"
    typeset FALSE="${FALSE:-1}"
    typeset VERBOSE="${VERBOSE:-${FALSE}}"
    typeset VERYVERB="${VERYVERB:-${FALSE}}"
    typeset OPTIND="1"
    typeset CMD_ECHO="${GBL_ECHO:-echo -e }"
    typeset MYT_PROGRAM="my_template02_zbksh"
    typeset MYT_VERSION="1.0"
    typeset MYT_TGGLEUP="${FALSE}"
    typeset MYT_TGGLELO="${FALSE}"
    typeset MYT_ARGVALU=""

#### Call the configuration function and execute the configuration file.

    configure_my_template02_zbksh "${MYT_PROGRAM}"

#### Process the command line options and arguments.

    while getopts ":vvul" OPTION
    do
        case "${OPTION}" in
            'u') MYT_TGGLEUP="${TRUE}";;
            'l') MYT_TGGLELO="${TRUE}";;
            'v') VERBOSE="${TRUE}";;
            'v') VERYVERB="${TRUE}";;
            '?') usagemsg_my_template02_zbksh "${MYT_PROGRAM}" "${MYT_VERSION}"
&& return 1 ;;
            ':') usagemsg_my_template02_zbksh "${MYT_PROGRAM}" "${MYT_VERSION}"
&& return 2 ;;
            '#') usagemsg_my_template02_zbksh "${MYT_PROGRAM}" "${MYT_VERSION}"
&& return 3 ;;
        esac
    done

    shift $(( ${OPTIND} - 1 ))

#################################################

#### Place any command line option error checking statements
#### here.  If an error is detected, print a message to
#### standard error, and return from this function with a
```

```ksh
#### non-zero return code.  The "trap" statement will cause
#### the "usagemsg" to be displayed.

   trap "usagemsg_my_template02_zbksh ${MYT_PROGRAM} ${MYT_VERSION}" EXIT

   if (( MYT_TGGLEUP == TRUE )) &&
      (( MYT_TGGLELO == TRUE ))
   then
        ${CMD_ECHO} "# ERROR: Do not specify both upper and lower case conversion
together"
        return 11
   fi

   trap "-" EXIT

##################################################

   (( VERYVERB == TRUE )) && set -x
   (( VERBOSE  == TRUE )) && ${CMD_ECHO} "# Program Name......: ${MYT_PROGRAM}"
   (( VERBOSE  == TRUE )) && ${CMD_ECHO} "# Version...........: ${MYT_VERSION}"

   for MYT_ARGVALU in "${@}"
   do
        (( VERBOSE  == TRUE )) && ${CMD_ECHO} "# Command Line Arg..:
${MYT_ARGVALU}"
   done

##################################################

####
#### Your shell function should perform its specific work here.
#### All work performed by your shell function should be coded
#### within this section of the function.  This does not mean that
#### your function should be called from here, it means the shell
#### code that performs the work of your function should be
#### incorporated into the body of this function.  This should
#### become your function.
####

   if (( ${#@} > 0 ))
   then
        MYT_MSG="${@}"
   fi

   if [[ "_${MYT_MSG}" != "_" ]]
   then
        (( MYT_TGGLEUP == TRUE )) && typeset -u MYT_MSG="${MYT_MSG}"
        (( MYT_TGGLELO == TRUE )) && typeset -l MYT_MSG="${MYT_MSG}"

        (( VERBOSE  == TRUE )) && ${CMD_ECHO} "# MYT_MSG Variable Value:
${MYT_MSG}"
        ${CMD_ECHO} "${MYT_MSG}"
   fi

#### If you need to define array values inside a while or until loop, and you
#### read input from a file, redirect input into the while loop instead of
#### using a pipe. Bash requires this syntax if you need the array values to
#### be visible outside of the loop.
####
#### Example Syntax:
####    grep X file > /tmp/tmp${$}.out
####    IDX="0"
####    while read VALUE
####    do ARRY[IDX++]="${VALUE}"
####    done < /tmp/tmp${$}.out
####    rm -f /tmp/tmp${$}.out
####    for i in "${ARRY[@]}"; do echo ${i}; done
####

   return 0
}
##################################################
```

```
################################################
################################################
####
#### Main Body of Script Begins Here
####
################################################

TRUE="0"
FALSE="1"

####
#### Extract the "shebang" line from the beginning of the script

read SHEBANG < "${0}"
export SHEBANG

####
#### Test the "shebang" line to determine what shell interpreter is specified

SHCODE="unknown"
[[ "_${SHEBANG}" == _*/ksh*  ]] && SHCODE="korn"
[[ "_${SHEBANG}" == _*/bash* ]] && SHCODE="bash"
[[ "_${SHEBANG}" == _*/zsh*  ]] && SHCODE="zshell"
export SHCODE

####
#### Modify the commands and script according to the shell interpreter

GBL_ECHO="echo -e"
[[ "_${SHCODE}" == "_korn"   ]] && GBL_ECHO="print --"
[[ "_${SHCODE}" == "_zshell" ]] && GBL_ECHO="print --" && emulate ksh93
[[ "_${SHCODE}" == "_bash"   ]] && shopt -s extglob   # Turn on extended
globbing

####
#### Call the script function to begin processing

my_template02_zbksh "${@}"
```

Appendix C

Function: my_template03_zbksh

```
#!/usr/bin/ksh93
#!/bin/bash
#!/bin/zsh
##################################################
####
#### This script will run in KornShell193, Zshell, or Bash, all you need to do
#### is put the desired "shebang" line at the top of the script.
####
##################################################
function usagemsg_my_template03_zbksh {

    stderr_zbksh ""
    stderr_zbksh "${1:+Program: ${1}}${2:+          Version: ${2}}"
    stderr_zbksh ""
    stderr_zbksh "Place a brief description ( < 255 chars ) of your shell"
    stderr_zbksh "function here."
    stderr_zbksh ""
    stderr_zbksh "Usage: ${1##*/} [-?vV] [-u] [-l]"
    stderr_zbksh ""
    stderr_zbksh "  where:"
    stderr_zbksh "    -u = Convert command line arguments to upper case"
    stderr_zbksh "    -l = Convert command line arguments to lower case"
    stderr_zbksh "    -v = Verbose mode - displays function info"
    stderr_zbksh "    -V = Very Verbose Mode - debug output displayed"
    stderr_zbksh "    -? = Help - display this message"
    stderr_zbksh ""
    stderr_zbksh "Author: Your Name (YourEmail@address.com)"
    stderr_zbksh ""
    stderr_zbksh "\"AutoContent\" enabled"
    stderr_zbksh "\"Multi-Shell\" enabled"
    stderr_zbksh ""

}
##################################################
####
#### Description:
####
#### Place a full text description of your shell function here.
####
#### Assumptions:
####
#### Provide a list of assumptions your shell function makes,
#### with a description of each assumption.
####
#### Dependencies:
####
#### Provide a list of dependencies your shell function has,
#### with a description of each dependency.
####
#### Products:
####
#### Provide a list of output your shell function produces,
#### with a description of each product.
####
#### Configured Usage:
####
#### Describe how your shell function should be used.
####
#### Details:
####
#### Place nothing here, the details are your shell function.
####
```

```
##################################################
configure_my_template03_zbksh()
{
####
#### Notice this function is a POSIX function so that it can see local
#### and global variables from calling functions and scripts.
####
#### Configuration parameters can be stored in a file and
#### this script can be dynamically reconfigured by sending
#### the running script a HUP signal using the kill command.
####
#### Configuration variables can be defined in the configuration file using
#### the same syntax as defining a shell variable, e.g.: VARIABLE="value"

    [[ "_${1}" != "_" ]] && MYT_CFILE=~/.${1}.conf

    (( VERBOSE == TRUE )) && stderr_zbksh "# Configuration File: ${MYT_CFILE}"

    if [[ -f ${MYT_CFILE} ]]
    then
        (( VERBOSE == TRUE )) && cat ${MYT_CFILE}
        . ${MYT_CFILE}
    fi

    return 0
}
##################################################
function my_template03_zbksh {

    typeset TRUE="${TRUE:-0}"
    typeset FALSE="${FALSE:-1}"
    typeset VERBOSE="${VERBOSE:-${FALSE}}"
    typeset VERYVERB="${VERYVERB:-${FALSE}}"
    typeset OPTIND="1"
    typeset MYT_PROGRAM="my_template03_zbksh"
    typeset MYT_VERSION="1.0"
    typeset MYT_TGGLEUP="${FALSE}"
    typeset MYT_TGGLELO="${FALSE}"
    typeset MYT_ARGVALU=""

#### Call the configuration function and execute the configuration file.

    configure_my_template03_zbksh "${MYT_PROGRAM}"

#### Process the command line options and arguments.

    while getopts ":vvul" OPTION
    do
        case "${OPTION}" in
            'u') MYT_TGGLEUP="${TRUE}";;
            'l') MYT_TGGLELO="${TRUE}";;
            'v') VERBOSE="${TRUE}";;
            'V') VERYVERB="${TRUE}";;
            '?') usagemsg_my_template03_zbksh "${MYT_PROGRAM}" "${MYT_VERSION}"
&& return 1 ;;
            ':') usagemsg_my_template03_zbksh "${MYT_PROGRAM}" "${MYT_VERSION}"
&& return 2 ;;
            '#') usagemsg_my_template03_zbksh "${MYT_PROGRAM}" "${MYT_VERSION}"
&& return 3 ;;
        esac
    done

    shift $(( ${OPTIND} - 1 ))

##################################################

#### Place any command line option error checking statements
#### here.  If an error is detected, print a message to
#### standard error, and return from this function with a
#### non-zero return code.  The "trap" statement will cause
#### the "usagemsg" to be displayed.
```

```
    trap "usagemsg_my_template03_zbksh ${MYT_PROGRAM} ${MYT_VERSION}" EXIT

    if (( MYT_TGGLEUP == TRUE )) &&
       (( MYT_TGGLELO == TRUE ))
    then
        stderr_zbksh "# ERROR: Do not specify both upper and lower case
conversion together"
        return 11
    fi

    trap "-" EXIT

    ##################################################

    (( VERYVERB == TRUE )) && set -x
    (( VERBOSE  == TRUE )) && stderr_zbksh "# Program Name..........:
${MYT_PROGRAM}"
    (( VERBOSE  == TRUE )) && stderr_zbksh "# Version...............:
${MYT_VERSION}"

    for MYT_ARGVALU in "${@}"
    do
        (( VERBOSE  == TRUE )) && stderr_zbksh "# Command Line Arg......:
${MYT_ARGVALU}"
    done

    ##################################################

    ####
    #### Your shell function should perform its specific work here.
    #### All work performed by your shell function should be coded
    #### within this section of the function.  This does not mean that
    #### your function should be called from here, it means the shell
    #### code that performs the work of your function should be
    #### incorporated into the body of this function.  This should
    #### become your function.
    ####

    if (( ${#@} > 0 ))
    then
        MYT_MSG="${@}"
    fi

    if [[ "_${MYT_MSG}" != "_" ]]
    then
        (( MYT_TGGLEUP == TRUE )) && typeset -u MYT_MSG="${MYT_MSG}"
        (( MYT_TGGLELO == TRUE )) && typeset -l MYT_MSG="${MYT_MSG}"

        (( VERBOSE  == TRUE )) && stderr_zbksh "# MYT_MSG Variable Value:
${MYT_MSG}"
        stdout_zbksh "${MYT_MSG}"
    fi

    #### If you need to define array values inside a while or until loop, and you
    #### read input from a file, redirect input into the while loop instead of
    #### using a pipe. Bash requires this syntax if you need the array values to
    #### be visible outside of the loop.
    ####
    #### Example Syntax:
    ####     grep X file > /tmp/tmp${$}.out
    ####     IDX="0"
    ####     while read VALUE
    ####     do ARRY[IDX++]="${VALUE}"
    ####     done < /tmp/tmp${$}.out
    ####     rm -f /tmp/tmp${$}.out
    ####     for i in "${ARRY[@]}"; do echo ${i}; done
    ####

    return 0
}
##################################################
##################################################
```

```
#################################################
####
#### Main Body of Script Begins Here
####
#################################################

####
#### Identify the function library directories to search
#### in the FPATH environment variable

FPATH=~/functions/adv_zbksh:~/functions:/usr/local/functions
export FPATH

####
#### Define the values for TRUE and FALSE,
#### In shell think, TRUE is zero (0) and FALSE is non-zero.

TRUE="0"
FALSE="1"

####
#### Extract the "shebang" line from the beginning of the script

read SHEBANG < "${0}"
export SHEBANG

####
#### Test the "shebang" line to determine what shell interpreter is specified

SHCODE="unknown"
[[ "_${SHEBANG}" == _*/ksh* ]] && SHCODE="korn"
[[ "_${SHEBANG}" == _*/bash* ]] && SHCODE="bash"
[[ "_${SHEBANG}" == _*/zsh* ]] && SHCODE="zshell"
export SHCODE

####
#### Modify the shell specific commands and script according to the shell
interpreter

GBL_ECHO="echo -e"
[[ "_${SHCODE}" == "_korn" ]] && GBL_ECHO="print --"
[[ "_${SHCODE}" == "_zshell" ]] && GBL_ECHO="print --" && emulate ksh93
[[ "_${SHCODE}" == "_bash" ]] && shopt -s extglob    # Turn on extended
globbing

####
#### For those shell interpreters that do not directly support function
libraries,
#### cache all the *_zbksh functions found in the FPATH directories.
####

if [[ "_${SHCODE}" == "_zshell" ]] ||
   [[ "_${SHCODE}" == "_bash"   ]]
then

#### Loop thru each directory in the FPATH list using a colon (:) delimeter.
#### Process each directory in reverse order to simulate results of
#### searching the FPATH directory.

    IFS=":"
    FDIRS=( ${FPATH} )
    IFS=$' \t\n'

    END=${#FDIRS[@]}
    for (( IDX=END-1; IDX>=0; --IDX ))
    do
        FDIR="${FDIRS[${IDX}]}"

#### Gather a list of functions ending in *_zbksh from the directory and loop
#### thru each file using a "for" loop.

        for FUNC in ${FDIR}/*_zbksh
```

```
        do
####
#### Check each *_zbksh file to see if it starts with a function, if so
#### cache it in the current environment by running it as as a "dot" script.
####
            if head -1 "${FUNC}" 2>/dev/null | egrep 'function|\(\)' >
/dev/null 2>&1
            then
                . "${FUNC}"
            fi
        done
    done

    IFS=$' \t\n'

fi


####
#### Call the script function to begin processing

my_template03_zbksh "${@}"
```

Appendix D

Function Library

Function: echo_zbksh

```
function echo_zbksh {
#################################################

    typeset PROGRAM="echo_zbksh"
    typeset VERSION="1.0"
    typeset TRUE="0"
    typeset FALSE="1"
    typeset VERBOSE="${FALSE}"
    typeset VERYVERB="${FALSE}"
    typeset OPTIND="1"
    typeset FDNUM="1"
    typeset RETCODE="99"
    typeset CMD_ECHO="${GBL_ECHO:-echo -e }"


#################################################

    find_dot_file_zbksh -f "echo_zbksh" -a "configure"

#################################################

####
#### Process the command line options and arguments, saving
#### the values as appropriate.
####

    while getopts ":vVDEu:" OPTION
    do
        case "${OPTION}" in
            'u') FDNUM="${OPTARG}";;
            'v') VERBOSE="${TRUE}";;
            'V') VERYVERB="${TRUE}";;
            'D') find_dot_file_zbksh -f "${PROGRAM}" -a "document" && return 4;;
            'E') find_dot_file_zbksh -f "${PROGRAM}" -a "example"  && return 5;;
            '?') find_dot_file_zbksh -f "${PROGRAM}" -a "usagemsg" && return 1 ;;
            ':') find_dot_file_zbksh -f "${PROGRAM}" -a "usagemsg" && return 2 ;;
            '#') find_dot_file_zbksh -f "${PROGRAM}" -a "usagemsg" && return 3 ;;
        esac
    done

    shift $(( ${OPTIND} - 1 ))
    [[ "_${1}" == "_--" ]] && shift 1
    [[ "_${1}" == "_--" ]] && shift 1
    [[ "_${1}" == "_--" ]] && shift 1

####
#### Check the command line arguments to verify they are valid values and that
all
#### necessary information was specified.
####

    trap "find_dot_file_zbksh -f echo_zbksh -a usagemsg" EXIT

    if [[ "_${FDNUM}" == "_" ]]
    then
        stderr_zbksh -- "# ERROR: File Descriptor number not specified"
        return 2
```

```
    fi

    trap "-" EXIT

#################################################

####
#### Display some program info and the command line arguments specified
#### if "VERBOSE" mode was specified.
####

    (( VERYVERB == TRUE )) && set -x

    verbose_comment_zbksh -v "${VERBOSE}" -p "Program"          -a "${PROGRAM}"
    verbose_comment_zbksh -v "${VERBOSE}" -p "Version"          -a "${VERSION}"
    verbose_comment_zbksh -v "${VERBOSE}" -p "File Descriptor" -a "${FDNUM}"

#################################################

    RETCODE="0"
    if (( FDNUM == 1 ))
    then
        eval ${CMD_ECHO} "\"${@}\""
        RETCODE="${?}"
    fi

    if (( FDNUM == 2 ))
    then
        eval ${CMD_ECHO} "\"${@}\"" >&2
        RETCODE="${?}"
    fi

    return ${RETCODE}

}
####
#### #################################################
```

Function: execl_zbksh

```
function execl_zbksh {
#### #################################################

    typeset PROGRAM="execl_zbksh"
    typeset VERSION="1.0"
    typeset TRUE="0"
    typeset FALSE="1"
    typeset VERBOSE="${FALSE}"
    typeset VERYVERB="${FALSE}"
    typeset OPTIND="1"
    typeset OPT_SSH="-o UserKnownHostsFile=/dev/null -o StrictHostKeyChecking=no
-o LogLevel=quiet -o BatchMode=yes -o ConnectTimeout=30"
    typeset CMD_SSH="ssh"
    typeset SSHPORT=22
    typeset SSHUSER="sshuser"
    typeset SSHADDR=""
    typeset RETCODE="99"

#################################################

    find_dot_file_zbksh -f "execl_zbksh" -a "configure"

#################################################

####
#### Process the command line options and arguments, saving
#### the values as appropriate.
####
```

```
while getopts ":vVDEp:u:a:" OPTION
do
    case "${OPTION}" in
        'p')  SSHPORT="${OPTARG}";;
        'u')  SSHUSER="${OPTARG}";;
        'a')  SSHADDR="${OPTARG}";;
        'v')  VERBOSE="${TRUE}";;
        'V')  VERYVERB="${TRUE}";;
        'D')  find_dot_file_zbksh -f "${PROGRAM}" -a "document" && return 4;;
        'E')  find_dot_file_zbksh -f "${PROGRAM}" -a "example"  && return 5;;
        '?')  find_dot_file_zbksh -f "${PROGRAM}" -a "usagemsg" && return 1 ;;
        ':')  find_dot_file_zbksh -f "${PROGRAM}" -a "usagemsg" && return 2 ;;
        '#')  find_dot_file_zbksh -f "${PROGRAM}" -a "usagemsg" && return 3 ;;
    esac
done

shift $(( ${OPTIND} - 1 ))
[[ "_${1}" == "_--" ]] && shift 1
[[ "_${1}" == "_--" ]] && shift 1
[[ "_${1}" == "_--" ]] && shift 1

##################################################

####
#### Check the command line arguments to verify they are valid values and that all
#### necessary information was specified.
####

    trap "find_dot_file_zbksh -f execl_zbksh -a usagemsg" EXIT

    if [[ "_${SSHADDR}" != "_" ]] &&
       [[ "_${SSHPORT}" == "_" ]]
    then
        stderr_zbksh -- "# ERROR: SSH Port not specified"
        return 10
    fi

    if [[ "_${SSHADDR}" != "_" ]] &&
       [[ "_${SSHUSER}" == "_" ]]
    then
        stderr_zbksh -- "# ERROR: SSH User not specified"
        return 11
    fi

    trap "-" EXIT

##################################################

#### Define the command execution mode, either local or remote depending upon
#### the value of the SSHADDR variable. If it contains a remote IP address or
#### hostname, define the execution mode variable. Otherwise it are set to
#### NULL, which means the commands will run locally.

    EXECMODE="${SSHADDR:+${CMD_SSH} ${OPT_SSH} -p ${SSHPORT} ${SSHUSER}@${SSHADDR}}"

    verbose_comment_zbksh -v "${VERBOSE}" -c "${EXECMODE:-eval} \"${@}\""

    ${EXECMODE:-eval} "${@}"
    RETCODE="${?}"

    return ${RETCODE}

}
####
#### ##################################################
```

Function: find_dot_file_zbksh

```
find_dot_file_zbksh()
#### ##############################################
{
  typeset DOT_PROGRAM="find_dot_file_zbksh"
  typeset DOT_VERSION="1.0"
  typeset DOT_TRUE="0"
  typeset DOT_FALSE="1"
  typeset DOT_VERBOSE="${DOT_VERBOSE:-${DOT_FALSE}}"
  typeset DOT_VERYVERB="${DOT_VERYVERB:-${DOT_FALSE}}"
  typeset OPTIND="1"
  typeset DOT_FUNCNAME="find_dot_file_zbksh"
  typeset DOT_ACTION="usagemsg"
  typeset DOT_EXTFILE="./.find_dot_file_zbksh.usagemsg"
  typeset DOT_RETCODE="99"
  typeset DOT_DIR
  typeset DOT_LINE
  typeset DOT_RECURS="${DOT_RECURS:-${TRUE}}"

##################################################

  if  (( DOT_RECURS == DOT_TRUE ))
  then
      DOT_RECURS="${DOT_FALSE}"
      find_dot_file_zbksh -f "find_dot_file_zbksh" -a "configure"
  else
      DOT_RECURS="${DOT_TRUE}"
      return 0
  fi

##################################################

####
#### Process the command line options and arguments, saving
#### the values as appropriate.
####

  while getopts ":vVDEf:a:" OPTION
  do
    DOT_OPTIND="${OPTIND}"
    case "${OPTION}" in
     'f') DOT_FUNCNAME="${OPTARG}";;
     'a') DOT_ACTION="${OPTARG}";;
     'v') DOT_VERBOSE="${DOT_TRUE}";;
     'V') DOT_VERYVERB="${DOT_TRUE}";;
     'D') find_dot_file_zbksh -f "${DOT_PROGRAM}" -a "document" && return 4;;
     'E') find_dot_file_zbksh -f "${DOT_PROGRAM}" -a "example"  && return 5;;
     '?') find_dot_file_zbksh -f "${DOT_PROGRAM}" -a "usagemsg" && return 1 ;;
     ':') find_dot_file_zbksh -f "${DOT_PROGRAM}" -a "usagemsg" && return 2 ;;
     '#') find_dot_file_zbksh -f "${DOT_PROGRAM}" -a "usagemsg" && return 3 ;;
    esac
    OPTIND="${DOT_OPTIND}"
  done

  shift $(( ${OPTIND} - 1 ))

  (( DOT_VERYVERB == DOT_TRUE )) && set -x

##################################################
####
#### Check the command line arguments to verify they are valid values and that all
#### necessary information was specified.
####

#   trap "find_dot_file_zbksh -f find_dot_file_zbksh -a usagemsg" EXIT

  if [[ "_${DOT_FUNCNAME}" == "_" ]]
  then
```

```
#        verbose_comment_zbksh -v "${DOT_VERBOSE}" -c "ERROR: Function Name not
specified"
       return 10
   fi

   if [[ "_${DOT_ACTION}" != _[Cc][Oo][Nn][Ff][Ii][Gg][Uu][Rr][Ee] ]] &&
      [[ "_${DOT_ACTION}" != _[Uu][Ss][Aa][Gg][Ee][Mm][Ss][Gg]    ]] &&
      [[ "_${DOT_ACTION}" == _[Dd][Oo][Cc][Uu][Mm][Ee][Nn][Tt]    ]] &&
      [[ "_${DOT_ACTION}" == _[Ee][Xx][Aa][Mm][Pp][Ll][Ee]        ]]
   then
       stderr_comment_zbksh -p "ERROR: Invalid Action Specified" -a
"${DOT_ACTION}"
       find_dot_file_zbksh -f "find_dot_file_zbksh" -a "usagemsg"
       return 11
   fi

#   trap "-" EXIT

#################################################

####
#### Display some DOT_PROGRAM info and the command line arguments specified
#### if "DOT_VERBOSE" mode was specified.
####

   (( DOT_VERYVERB == DOT_TRUE )) && set -x
#    verbose_comment_zbksh -v "${DOT_VERBOSE}" -p "Program"       -a
"${DOT_PROGRAM}"
#    verbose_comment_zbksh -v "${DOT_VERBOSE}" -p "Version"       -a
"${DOT_VERSION}"
#    verbose_comment_zbksh -v "${DOT_VERBOSE}" -p "Function Name" -a
"${DOT_FUNCNAME}"
#    verbose_comment_zbksh -v "${DOT_VERBOSE}" -p "Action"        -a
"${DOT_ACTION}"

#################################################
####
####
####

   DOT_RETCODE="0"

#################################################

#### Define the possible directory locations for the "dot" files in the FPATH
directories.

   IDX="0"
   IFS=$': \t\n'
   for DIR in ${FPATH}
   do
       DOT_FPATHS[IDX++]="${DIR}"
   done
   IFS=$' \t\n'

#################################################

#### Define the possible directory locations for the "dot" files under the
users HOME.

####     typeset DOT_HOMES[0]=~
####     typeset DOT_HOMES[1]=~/.adv_zbksh
####     typeset DOT_HOMES[2]=~/adv_zbksh
####     typeset DOT_HOMES[3]=~/functions/adv_zbksh
####     typeset DOT_HOMES[4]=~/functions

   IDX="0"
   DOT_HOMES[IDX++]=~
   DOT_HOMES[IDX++]=~/.adv_zbksh
   DOT_HOMES[IDX++]=~/adv_zbksh
   DOT_HOMES[IDX++]=~/functions/adv_zbksh
   DOT_HOMES[IDX++]=~/functions
```

```
#### Define the possible directory locations for the "dot" files under
/usr/local.

####    typeset DOT_LOCALS[0]="/usr/local/adv_zbksh"
####    typeset DOT_LOCALS[1]="/usr/local/functions/adv_zbksh"
####    typeset DOT_LOCALS[2]="/usr/local/functions"
####    typeset DOT_LOCALS[3]="/usr/local/scripts/adv_zbksh"
####    typeset DOT_LOCALS[4]="/usr/local/scripts"

  IDX="0"
  DOT_LOCALS[IDX++]="/usr/local/adv_zbksh"
  DOT_LOCALS[IDX++]="/usr/local/functions/adv_zbksh"
  DOT_LOCALS[IDX++]="/usr/local/functions"
  DOT_LOCALS[IDX++]="/usr/local/scripts/adv_zbksh"
  DOT_LOCALS[IDX++]="/usr/local/scripts"

#### Define the possible directory locations for the "dot" files under MAN
pages.

####    typeset DOT_MANS[0]="/usr/share/man/man1"
  IDX="0"
  DOT_MANS[IDX++]="/usr/share/man/man1"

#### Define the "dot" file name extensions based on the CLI action specified.

  [[ "_${DOT_ACTION}" == _[Cc][Oo][Nn][Ff][Ii][Gg][Uu][Rr][Ee] ]] &&
DOT_EXTENSION=".conf"
  [[ "_${DOT_ACTION}" == _[Uu][Ss][Aa][Gg][Ee][Mm][Ss][Gg]      ]] &&
DOT_EXTENSION=".usagemsg"
  [[ "_${DOT_ACTION}" == _[Dd][Oo][Cc][Uu][Mm][Ee][Nn][Tt]      ]] &&
DOT_EXTENSION=".usagemsg"
  [[ "_${DOT_ACTION}" == _[Ee][Xx][Aa][Mm][Pp][Ll][Ee]          ]] &&
DOT_EXTENSION=".usagemsg"

#   verbose_comment_zbksh -v "${DOT_VERBOSE}" -p "File Extension" -a
"${DOT_EXTENSION}"

#### Loop through each of the directory locations searching for the first
occurrence of
#### a matching "dot" file. The directories are search in order of HOMES,
LOCALS, MANS.
#### The first "dot" file found cause the loop to break.

  for DOT_DIR in "${DOT_FPATHS[@]}" "${DOT_HOMES[@]}" "${DOT_LOCALS[@]}"
"${DOT_MANS[@]}"
  do
    if [[ -f "${DOT_DIR}/.${DOT_FUNCNAME}${DOT_EXTENSION}" ]]
    then
      DOT_EXTFILE="${DOT_DIR}/.${DOT_FUNCNAME}${DOT_EXTENSION}"
#       verbose_comment_zbksh -v "${DOT_VERBOSE}" -p "External File Found" -a
"${DOT_EXTFILE}"
      break
    fi
  done

#### If an external dot file exists, and the action is "configure", then
#### execute the file as a "dot" script in the current environment

  if [[    "_${DOT_EXTFILE}" != "_"      ]] &&
     [[    "_${DOT_EXTFILE}" == _*.conf  ]] &&
     [[ -f "${DOT_EXTFILE}"              ]] &&
     [[    "_${DOT_ACTION}"  == _[Cc][Oo][Nn][Ff][Ii][Gg][Uu][Rr][Ee] ]]
  then
    . ${DOT_EXTFILE}
#     verbose_comment_zbksh -v "${DOT_VERBOSE}" -p "Executing dot script" -a
"${DOT_EXTFILE}"
  fi

#### If an external dot file exists, and the action is "usagemsg", then
#### display the file on STDERR as a usage message.
```

```
if [[    "_${DOT_EXTFILE}" != "_"            ]] &&
   [[    "_${DOT_EXTFILE}" == _*.usagemsg    ]] &&
   [[ -f "${DOT_EXTFILE}"                    ]] &&
   [[    "_${DOT_ACTION}"  == _[Uu][Ss][Aa][Gg][Ee][Mm][Ss][Gg]    ]] ]]
then
#      verbose_comment_zbksh -v "${DOT_VERBOSE}" -p "Displaying dot script" -a
"${DOT_EXTFILE}"
       while IFS="" read -r -- DOT_LINE
       do
              stderr_zbksh -- "${DOT_LINE}"
       done < "${DOT_EXTFILE}"
    fi

#### If an external dot file exists, and the action is "document", then
#### display usagemsg, comments, and examples on STDOUT.

    if [[    "_${DOT_EXTFILE}" != "_"            ]] &&
       [[    "_${DOT_EXTFILE}" == _*.usagemsg    ]] &&
       [[ -f "${DOT_EXTFILE}"                    ]] &&
       [[    "_${DOT_ACTION}"  == _[Dd][Oo][Cc][Uu][Mm][Ee][Nn][Tt]    ]] ]]
    then
       while IFS="" read -r -- DOT_LINE
       do
              stdout_zbksh -- "${DOT_LINE}"
       done < "${DOT_EXTFILE}"

       grep '^#### ' ${DOT_FUNCNAME} | sed -e 's/^#### //g'
    fi

#### If an external dot file exists, and the action is "example", then
#### execute the function examples and display the results on STDOUT.

    if    [[    "_${DOT_EXTFILE}" != "_" ]] &&
          [[ -f "${DOT_EXTFILE}"         ]] &&
     (    [[    "_${DOT_ACTION}"  == _[Dd][Oo][Cc][Uu][Mm][Ee][Nn][Tt] ]] ||
          [[    "_${DOT_ACTION}"  == _[Ee][Xx][Aa][Mm][Pp][Ll][Ee]     ]] )
    then
        IFS=$'\n'

        sed -e '/Example Usage:/,/^$/ !d' ${DOT_EXTFILE} > /tmp/tmp${$}.example
        IDX=0
        while read LINE
        do
            DOT_EXAMPLES[IDX++]="${LINE}"
        done < /tmp/tmp${$}.example
        rm -f /tmp/tmp${$}.example
        DOT_EXAMPLES[0]=''

        IFS=$' \t\n'

        for DOT_EXAMPLE in "${DOT_EXAMPLES[@]}"
        do
            [[ "_${DOT_EXAMPLE}" == "_" ]] && continue
            [[ "_${SHCODE}" == "_korn" ]] && set -x
               eval ${DOT_EXAMPLE}
            [[ "_${SHCODE}" == "_korn" ]] && set +x
        done
    fi

    OPTIND="1"

    return 0
}
####
#### ##################################################
```

Function: stderr_comment_zbksh

```
function stderr_comment_zbksh {
#### ##############################################

    typeset PROGRAM="stderr_comment_zbksh"
    typeset VERSION="1.0"
    typeset TRUE="0"
    typeset FALSE="1"
    typeset VERBOSE="${TRUE}"
    typeset VERYVERB="${FALSE}"
    typeset PROMPT_STRING=""
    typeset ANSWER_STRING=""
    typeset COMMENT_FIRST=""
    typeset COMMENT_LAST=""
    typeset COMMENT_STRING=""
    typeset DELETE_STRING=""
    typeset PROMPT_WIDTH="40"
    typeset OPTIND="1"
    typeset RETCODE="99"
    typeset SECZI="0"
    typeset DOTCHAR="."


##############################################

    find_dot_file_zbksh -f "stderr_comment_zbksh" -a "configure"

    typeset DOTS=""
    typeset KPAT=""
    for (( SECZI=0; SECZI<=${PROMPT_WIDTH}; ++SECZI ))
    do
        DOTS="${DOTS}${DOTCHAR}"
        KPAT="${KPAT}?"
    done

##############################################

####
#### Process the command line options and arguments, saving
#### the values as appropriate.
####

    while getopts ":v:VDEp:a:c:C:w:d:" OPTION
    do
        case "${OPTION}" in
            'p') PROMPT_STRING="${OPTARG}";;
            'a') ANSWER_STRING="${OPTARG}";;
            'c') COMMENT_FIRST="${OPTARG}";;
            'C') COMMENT_LAST="${OPTARG}";;

            'd') DOTCHAR="${OPTARG}"
                DOTS=""
                KPAT=""
                for (( SECZI=0; SECZI<=${PROMPT_WIDTH}; ++SECZI ))
                do
                    DOTS="${DOTS}${DOTCHAR}"
                    KPAT="${KPAT}?"
                done;;

            'w') PROMPT_WIDTH="${OPTARG}"
                DOTS=""
                KPAT=""
                for (( SECZI=0; SECZI<=${PROMPT_WIDTH}; ++SECZI ))
                do
                    DOTS="${DOTS}${DOTCHAR}"
                    KPAT="${KPAT}?"
                done;;

            'v') VERBOSE="${TRUE}";;
            'V') VERYVERB="${TRUE}";;
            'D') find_dot_file_zbksh -f "${PROGRAM}" -a "document" && return 4;;
            'E') find_dot_file_zbksh -f "${PROGRAM}" -a "example"  && return 5;;
            '?') find_dot_file_zbksh -f "${PROGRAM}" -a "usagemsg" && return 1 ;;
            ':') find_dot_file_zbksh -f "${PROGRAM}" -a "usagemsg" && return 2 ;;
```

```
            '#') find_dot_file_zbksh -f "${PROGRAM}" -a "usagemsg" && return 3 ;;
      esac
   done

   shift $(( ${OPTIND} - 1 ))
   [[ "_${1}" == "_--" ]] && shift 1
   [[ "_${1}" == "_--" ]] && shift 1
   [[ "_${1}" == "_--" ]] && shift 1

####
#### Check the command line arguments to verify they are valid values and that
all
#### necessary information was specified.
####

   trap "find_dot_file_zbksh -f stderr_zbksh -a usagemsg" EXIT

   trap "-" EXIT

#################################################

   (( VERYVERB == TRUE )) && set -x

#################################################

####
#### Display the comments as provided on the CLI.
####

   if [[ "_${COMMENT_FIRST}" != "_" ]]
   then
      COMMENT_STRING="# ${COMMENT_FIRST}"
      stderr_zbksh "${COMMENT_STRING}"
   fi

   if [[ "_${PROMPT_STRING}" != "_" ]] &&
      [[ "_${ANSWER_STRING}" != "_" ]]
   then

      PROMPT_STRING="${PROMPT_STRING}${DOTS}"
      DELETE_STRING="${PROMPT_STRING#$${KPAT}}"
      PROMPT_STRING="${PROMPT_STRING%$${DELETE_STRING}}"

      COMMENT_STRING="# ${PROMPT_STRING}: ${ANSWER_STRING}"
      stderr_zbksh "${COMMENT_STRING}"
   fi

   if [[ "_${COMMENT_LAST}" != "_" ]]
   then
      COMMENT_STRING="# ${COMMENT_LAST}"
      stderr_zbksh "${COMMENT_STRING}"
   fi

   RETCODE="0"

   return ${RETCODE}

}
####
#### #################################################
```

Function: stderr_zbksh

```
function stderr_zbksh {
#### #################################################

   typeset PROGRAM="stderr_zbksh"
   typeset VERSION="3.2"
```

```
    typeset TRUE="0"
    typeset FALSE="1"
    typeset VERBOSE="${FALSE}"
    typeset VERYVERB="${FALSE}"
    typeset OPTIND="1"
    typeset FDNUM="2"
    typeset RETCODE="99"

################################################

    find_dot_file_zbksh -f "stderr_zbksh" -a "configure"

################################################

####
#### Process the command line options and arguments, saving
#### the values as appropriate.
####

    while getopts ":vVDE" OPTION
    do
        case "${OPTION}" in
            'v') VERBOSE="${TRUE}";;
            'V') VERYVERB="${TRUE}";;
            'D') find_dot_file_zbksh -f "${PROGRAM}" -a "document" && return 4;;
            'E') find_dot_file_zbksh -f "${PROGRAM}" -a "example"  && return 5;;
            '?') find_dot_file_zbksh -f "${PROGRAM}" -a "usagemsg" && return 1 ;;
            ':') find_dot_file_zbksh -f "${PROGRAM}" -a "usagemsg" && return 2 ;;
            '#') find_dot_file_zbksh -f "${PROGRAM}" -a "usagemsg" && return 3 ;;
        esac
    done

    shift $(( ${OPTIND} - 1 ))
    [[ "_${1}" == "_--" ]] && shift 1
    [[ "_${1}" == "_--" ]] && shift 1
    [[ "_${1}" == "_--" ]] && shift 1

####
#### Check the command line arguments to verify they are valid values and that all
#### necessary information was specified.
####

    trap "find_dot_file_zbksh -f stderr_zbksh -a usagemsg" EXIT

    trap "-" EXIT

################################################

####
#### Display some program info and the command line arguments specified
#### if "VERBOSE" mode was specified.
####

    (( VERYVERB == TRUE )) && set -x

    verbose_comment_zbksh -v "${VERBOSE}" -p "Program"    -a "${PROGRAM}"
    verbose_comment_zbksh -v "${VERBOSE}" -p "Version"    -a "${VERSION}"

################################################

    echo_zbksh -u ${FDNUM} -- "${@}"
    RETCODE="${?}"

    return ${RETCODE}

}
####
#### ################################################
```

Function: stdout_zbksh

```
function stdout_zbksh {
#### #############################################

    typeset PROGRAM="stdout_zbksh"
    typeset VERSION="1.0"
    typeset TRUE="0"
    typeset FALSE="1"
    typeset VERBOSE="${FALSE}"
    typeset VERYVERB="${FALSE}"
    typeset OPTIND="1"
    typeset FDNUM="1"
    typeset RETCODE="99"


#################################################

    find_dot_file_zbksh -f "stdout_zbksh" -a "configure"

#################################################

####
#### Process the command line options and arguments, saving
#### the values as appropriate.
####

    while getopts ":vVDE" OPTION
    do
        case "${OPTION}" in
            'v') VERBOSE="${TRUE}";;
            'V') VERYVERB="${TRUE}";;
            'D') find_dot_file_zbksh -f "${PROGRAM}" -a "document" && return 4;;
            'E') find_dot_file_zbksh -f "${PROGRAM}" -a "example"  && return 5;;
            '?') find_dot_file_zbksh -f "${PROGRAM}" -a "usagemsg" && return 1 ;;
            ':') find_dot_file_zbksh -f "${PROGRAM}" -a "usagemsg" && return 2 ;;
            '#') find_dot_file_zbksh -f "${PROGRAM}" -a "usagemsg" && return 3 ;;
        esac
    done

    shift $(( ${OPTIND} - 1 ))
    [[ "_${1}" == "_--" ]] && shift 1
    [[ "_${1}" == "_--" ]] && shift 1
    [[ "_${1}" == "_--" ]] && shift 1

####
#### Check the command line arguments to verify they are valid values and that all
#### necessary information was specified.
####

    trap "find_dot_file_zbksh -f stderr_zbksh -a usagemsg" EXIT

    trap "-" EXIT

#################################################

####
#### Display some program info and the command line arguments specified
#### if "VERBOSE" mode was specified.
####

    (( VERYVERB == TRUE )) && set -x

    verbose_comment_zbksh -v "${VERBOSE}" -p "Program"   -a "${PROGRAM}"
    verbose_comment_zbksh -v "${VERBOSE}" -p "Version"   -a "${VERSION}"

#################################################

    echo_zbksh -u ${FDNUM} -- "${@}"
    RETCODE="${?}"
```

```
    return ${RETCODE}

}
####
#### ####################################################
```

Function: verbose_comment_zbksh

```
function verbose_comment_zbksh {
#### ####################################################

    typeset PROGRAM="verbose_comment_zbksh"
    typeset VERSION="1.0"
    typeset TRUE="0"
    typeset FALSE="1"
    typeset VERBOSE="${FALSE}"
    typeset TGGL_VERBOSE="${FALSE}"
    typeset VERYVERB="${FALSE}"
    typeset PROMPT_STRING=""
    typeset ANSWER_STRING=""
    typeset COMMENT_FIRST=""
    typeset COMMENT_LAST=""
    typeset PROMPT_WIDTH="40"
    typeset OPTIND="1"
    typeset RETCODE="99"

    #################################################

    find_dot_file_zbksh -v -f "verbose_comment_zbksh" -a "configure"

    #################################################

####
#### Process the command line options and arguments, saving
#### the values as appropriate.
####

    while getopts ":v:VDEp:a:c:C:w:" OPTION
    do
        case "${OPTION}" in
            'p') PROMPT_STRING="${OPTARG}";;
            'a') ANSWER_STRING="${OPTARG}";;
            'c') COMMENT_FIRST="${OPTARG}";;
            'C') COMMENT_LAST="${OPTARG}";;
            'w') PROMPT_WIDTH="${OPTARG}";;
            'v') TGGL_VERBOSE="${OPTARG}";;
            'V') VERYVERB="${TRUE}";;
            'D') find_dot_file_zbksh -f "${PROGRAM}" -a "document" && return 4;;
            'E') find_dot_file_zbksh -f "${PROGRAM}" -a "example"  && return 5;;
            '?') find_dot_file_zbksh -f "${PROGRAM}" -a "usagemsg" && return 1 ;;
            ':') find_dot_file_zbksh -f "${PROGRAM}" -a "usagemsg" && return 2 ;;
            '#') find_dot_file_zbksh -f "${PROGRAM}" -a "usagemsg" && return 3 ;;
        esac
    done

    shift $(( ${OPTIND} - 1 ))
    [[ "_${1}" == "_--" ]] && shift 1
    [[ "_${1}" == "_--" ]] && shift 1
    [[ "_${1}" == "_--" ]] && shift 1

####
#### Check the command line arguments to verify they are valid values and that all
#### necessary information was specified.
####

#    trap "find_dot_file_zbksh -f stderr_zbksh -a usagemsg" EXIT
```

```
#
#    trap "-" EXIT

#################################################

  (( TGGL_VERBOSE == FALSE )) && return 0

  (( VERYVERB == TRUE )) && set -x

#################################################

####
#### Display some program info and the command line arguments specified
#### if "VERBOSE" mode was specified.
####

  if (( TGGL_VERBOSE == TRUE ))
  then
      stderr_comment_zbksh ${COMMENT_FIRST:+-c "${COMMENT_FIRST}"}
${PROMPT_STRING:+-p "${PROMPT_STRING}"} ${ANSWER_STRING:+-a "${ANSWER_STRING}"}
${COMMENT_LAST:+-C "${COMMENT_LAST}"} -w ${PROMPT_WIDTH:-40}
  fi

  RETCODE="0"

  return ${RETCODE}

}
####
#### #################################################
```

Function: wikiAutoLoad_zbksh

```
function wikiAutoLoad_zbksh {

#### #################################################
####
#### Description:
####
#### The purpose of this program is to provide the shell programmer or system
#### administrator with an automated mechanism for uploading documentation
#### and content to a Mediawiki server.  This shell script can be run from
#### any system in an organization to automatically upload information to a
#### centralized wiki documentation server.
####
#### Assumptions:
####
#### It is assumed the content to be uploaded is stored in files on the local
#### system.  Each paged stored in a separate file. It is also assumed the
#### filename will be used as the Page title on the Wiki.  When the file name
#### is processed by this script, characters such as underscores "_", commas
#### ",", periods ".", dashes "-" are replaced with spaces, and the file
#### extension can be removed via a command line option.  So the user can
#### create files with names such as "My_Wiki_Page_to_Upload.html", and this
#### script will upload this file to a wiki page named "My Wiki Page to
#### Upload".
####
#### Dependencies:
####
#### This script requires the "wget" command to send files and receive
#### cookies from the Wiki Server.
####
#### Unix Utilities:
####     sed
####     rm
####
#### GNU Utilities:
####     wget
```

```
####
#### Products:
####
#### This script uploads the contents of a file and creates or updates a
#### Mediwiki pages on a Wiki Server.
####
#### Configured Usage:
####
#### This script can be run from the command line or included in a library
#### and called as a function.  One or more filenames containing content to
#### be uploaded to a Wiki Server must be specified on the command line or an
#### error is generated.
####
#### Page titles for single file uploads can be specified using the "-t"
#### command line option.  This option is only valid if a single file is
#### specified on the command line.
####
#### Bulk Uploads can be performed by specifying more than one filename on
#### the command line.  The page title for each page in a bulk upload will be
#### the filename containing the content.
####
#### Deleting File Extentions from page titles during Bulk file uploads:
#### Multiple file extensions can be specified for the "-e" option by using
#### the pipe "|" delimiter between each file extension.
####
#### Multiple Categories can be specified on the command line as an argument
#### to the "-C" option.  To specify multiple categories, separate each
#### category specified with a comma ",".
####
#### Details:
####
#################################################

    typeset PROGRAM="wikiAutoLoad_zbksh"
    typeset VERSION="2.0"
    typeset TRUE="0"
    typeset FALSE="1"
    typeset VERBOSE="${FALSE}"
    typeset VERYVERB="${FALSE}"

    typeset WAL_WIKIUSER="WikiSysop"
    typeset WAL_WIKIPASS="abcd1234"
    typeset WAL_APIURL="http://127.0.0.1/wiki/api.php"
    typeset WAL_PAGETITLE=""
    typeset WAL_CATEGORIES="Upload"
    typeset WAL_FILEEXTEN="html"
    typeset WAL_PRETAG="${FALSE}"
    typeset WAL_CONVERT="${FALSE}"

    typeset WAL_PREVIEW="${FALSE}"
    typeset WAL_DD_COOKIES="/home/dfrench/tmp"
    typeset WAL_DD_OUTFILE="/home/dfrench/tmp"
    typeset WAL_WGETOUT="${WAL_DD_OUTFILE}/wget${$}.out"

####
#### Process the command line options and arguments, saving
#### the values as appropriate.
####

    while getopts ":vVu:p:a:t:c:o:C:e:zfxDE" OPTION
    do
        case "${OPTION}" in
            'u') WAL_WIKIUSER="${OPTARG}";;
            'p') WAL_WIKIPASS="${OPTARG}";;
            'a') WAL_APIURL="${OPTARG}";;
            't') WAL_PAGETITLE="${OPTARG}";;
            'c') WAL_DD_COOKIES="${OPTARG}";;
            'o') WAL_DD_OUTFILE="${OPTARG}";;
            'C') WAL_CATEGORIES="${OPTARG}";;
            'e') WAL_FILEEXTEN="${OPTARG}";;
            'z') WAL_PREVIEW="${TRUE}";;
            'f') WAL_PRETAG="${TRUE}";;
```

```
                'x') WAL_CONVERT="${TRUE}";;
                'v') VERBOSE="${TRUE}";;
                'V') VERYVERB="${TRUE}";;
                'D') find_dot_file_zbksh -f "${PROGRAM}" -a "document" && return 4;;
                'E') find_dot_file_zbksh -f "${PROGRAM}" -a "example"  && return 5;;
                '?') find_dot_file_zbksh -f "${PROGRAM}" -a "usagemsg" && return 1 ;;
                ':') find_dot_file_zbksh -f "${PROGRAM}" -a "usagemsg" && return 2 ;;
                '#') find_dot_file_zbksh -f "${PROGRAM}" -a "usagemsg" && return 3 ;;
        esac
    done

    shift $(( ${OPTIND} - 1 ))

    trap "find_dot_file_zbksh -f ${PROGRAM} -a usagemsg" EXIT

    if (( ${#@} == 0 ))
    then
        stderr_comment_zbksh -c "# ERROR: Upload File(s) not specified"
        return 2
    fi

    if (( ${#@} > 1 )) && [[ "_${WAL_PAGETITLE}" != "_" ]]
    then
        stderr_comment_zbksh -c "# WARNING: More than one file was specified on the
command line."
        stderr_comment_zbksh -c "#          As a result the Page title, that was
also specified on"
        stderr_comment_zbksh -c "#          the command line, will not be used."
    fi

    trap "-" EXIT

####################################################

####
#### Display some program info and the command line arguments specified
#### if "VERBOSE" mode was specified.
####

    verbose_comment_zbksh -v "${VERBOSE}" -p "Program Name"    -a "${PROGRAM}"
    verbose_comment_zbksh -v "${VERBOSE}" -p "Version"         -a "
${VERSION}"
    verbose_comment_zbksh -v "${VERBOSE}" -p "True"            -a " ${TRUE}"
    verbose_comment_zbksh -v "${VERBOSE}" -p "False"           -a " ${FALSE}"
    verbose_comment_zbksh -v "${VERBOSE}" -p "WikiUser"        -a "
${WAL_WIKIUSER}"
    verbose_comment_zbksh -v "${VERBOSE}" -p "WikiPass"        -a "
${WAL_WIKIPASS}"
    verbose_comment_zbksh -v "${VERBOSE}" -p "API URL"         -a "
${WAL_APIURL}"
    verbose_comment_zbksh -v "${VERBOSE}" -p "Cookie Dir"      -a "
${WAL_DD_COOKIES}"
    verbose_comment_zbksh -v "${VERBOSE}" -p "Output Dir"      -a "
${WAL_DD_OUTFILE}"
    verbose_comment_zbksh -v "${VERBOSE}" -p "File Extension"  -a "
${WAL_FILEEXTEN}"

    (( VERBOSE   == TRUE )) && WAL_TORF="TRUE" || WAL_TORF="FALSE"
    verbose_comment_zbksh -v "${VERBOSE}" -p "Verbose Mode"  -a " ${WAL_TORF}"

    (( WAL_PREVIEW  == TRUE )) && WAL_TORF="TRUE" || WAL_TORF="FALSE"
    verbose_comment_zbksh -v "${VERBOSE}" -p "Preview Mode"  -a " ${WAL_TORF}"

    (( WAL_PRETAG   == TRUE )) && WAL_TORF="TRUE" || WAL_TORF="FALSE"
    verbose_comment_zbksh -v "${VERBOSE}" -p "Preformatted"  -a " ${WAL_TORF}"

    (( WAL_CONVERT  == TRUE )) && WAL_TORF="TRUE" || WAL_TORF="FALSE"
    verbose_comment_zbksh -v "${VERBOSE}" -p "Convert Chars" -a " ${WAL_TORF}"

####################################################
```

```
(( VERBOSE  == TRUE )) && stderr_comment_zbksh -v "${VERBOSE}" -p "Function"  -
a "wikiAutoLoad"
(( VERBOSE  == TRUE )) && stderr_comment_zbksh -v "${VERBOSE}" -p "====" -a
"===============" -d '='

##################################################
##################################################
##################################################
####
#### Retrieve a login token from the wikimedia server

(( VERBOSE  == TRUE )) && stderr_comment_zbksh -v "${VERBOSE}" -p "Function"  -
a "getWikiLoginToken_zbksh" -d '>'

#### getWikiLoginToken_zbksh   "${WAL_APIURL}" "${WAL_WIKIUSER}"
"${WAL_WIKIPASS}"

   typeset WAL_LGNAME="lgname=${WAL_WIKIUSER}"
   typeset WAL_LGPASS="lgpassword=${WAL_WIKIPASS}"
   typeset WAL_ACTION="action=login"
   typeset WAL_FORMAT="format=xml"
   typeset WAL_OUTFILE="${WAL_DD_OUTFILE}/loginToken${$}.xml"
   typeset WAL_SAVECOOKIES="${WAL_DD_COOKIES}/loginTokenCookies${$}.txt"

(( VERBOSE  == TRUE )) && stderr_comment_zbksh -v "${VERBOSE}" -p "Command" -a
"wget ${WAL_APIURL}" -d '>'

   WAL_GWLT_CMD="wget"
   WAL_GWLT_CMD=$( append_string_zbksh -1 "${WAL_GWLT_CMD}" -2 "-O
'${WAL_OUTFILE}'" )
   WAL_GWLT_CMD=$( append_string_zbksh -1 "${WAL_GWLT_CMD}" -2 "--save-cookies
'${WAL_SAVECOOKIES}'" )
   WAL_GWLT_CMD=$( append_string_zbksh -1 "${WAL_GWLT_CMD}" -2 "--keep-session-
cookies" )
   WAL_GWLT_CMD=$( append_string_zbksh -1 "${WAL_GWLT_CMD}" -2 "--post-
data='${WAL_ACTION}&${WAL_FORMAT}&${WAL_LGNAME}&${WAL_LGPASS}'" )
   WAL_GWLT_CMD=$( append_string_zbksh -1 "${WAL_GWLT_CMD}" -2 "'${WAL_APIURL}'"
)

   stdout_zbksh -- "${WAL_GWLT_CMD}"

   (( WAL_PREVIEW == FALSE )) && eval ${WAL_GWLT_CMD}

   if [[ -r "${WAL_OUTFILE}" ]]
   then
(( VERBOSE  == TRUE )) && stderr_comment_zbksh -v "${VERBOSE}" -p "wget output
file"  -a "${WAL_OUTFILE}" -d '>'
      WAL_LGTOKEN=$( < "${WAL_OUTFILE}" )
      WAL_LGTOKEN="${WAL_LGTOKEN#*token=\"}"
      WAL_LGTOKEN="${WAL_LGTOKEN%\"*}"
   else
(( VERBOSE  == TRUE )) && stderr_comment_zbksh -v "${VERBOSE}" -p "ERROR: wget
output file"  -a "${WAL_OUTFILE}" -d '>'
      return 10
   fi

(( VERBOSE  == TRUE )) && stderr_comment_zbksh -v "${VERBOSE}" -p
"getWikiLoginToken_zbksh LGTOKEN"  -a "${WAL_LGTOKEN}" -d '>'

(( VERBOSE  == TRUE )) && stderr_comment_zbksh -v "${VERBOSE}" -p "Function"  -
a "getWikiLoginToken_zbksh" -d '<'

####
#### Retrieve a login token from the wikimedia server
##################################################
##################################################
##################################################

(( VERBOSE  == TRUE )) && stderr_comment_zbksh -v "${VERBOSE}" -p "====" -a
"===============" -d '='

##################################################
```

```
##################################################
##################################################
####
#### Create a login session on the wikimedia server

(( VERBOSE  == TRUE )) && stderr_comment_zbksh -v "${VERBOSE}" -p "Function"  -
a "wikiAutoLoad"

####  mkWikiLoginSession_zbksh "${WAL_APIURL}" "${WAL_WIKIUSER}"
"${WAL_WIKIPASS}" "${WAL_LGTOKEN}"

(( VERBOSE  == TRUE )) && stderr_comment_zbksh -v "${VERBOSE}" -p "Function" -a
"mkWikiLoginSession_zbksh" -d '>'

  typeset WAL_LGNAME="lgname=${WAL_WIKIUSER}"
  typeset WAL_LGPASS="lgpassword=${WAL_WIKIPASS}"
  typeset WAL_LGTOKEN="lgtoken=${WAL_LGTOKEN}"

  typeset WAL_ACTION="action=login"
  typeset WAL_FORMAT="format=xml"
  typeset WAL_OUTFILE="${WAL_DD_OUTFILE}/wikiLogin${$}.xml"
  typeset WAL_LOADCOOKIES="${WAL_DD_COOKIES}/loginTokenCookies${$}.txt"
  typeset WAL_SAVECOOKIES="${WAL_DD_COOKIES}/editTokenCookies${$}.txt"

(( VERBOSE  == TRUE )) && stderr_comment_zbksh -v "${VERBOSE}" -p
"mkWikiLoginSession" -a "${WAL_WIKIUSER}" -d '>'

(( VERBOSE  == TRUE )) && stderr_comment_zbksh -v "${VERBOSE}" -p "Command" -a
"wget ${WAL_APIURL}" -d '>'

  WAL_MWLS_CMD="wget --debug --no-check-certificate"
  WAL_MWLS_CMD=$( append_string_zbksh -1 "${WAL_MWLS_CMD}" -2 "-o
'${WAL_OUTFILE}'" )
  WAL_MWLS_CMD=$( append_string_zbksh -1 "${WAL_MWLS_CMD}" -2 "--load-cookies
'${WAL_LOADCOOKIES}'" )
  WAL_MWLS_CMD=$( append_string_zbksh -1 "${WAL_MWLS_CMD}" -2 "--save-cookies
'${WAL_SAVECOOKIES}'" )
  WAL_MWLS_CMD=$( append_string_zbksh -1 "${WAL_MWLS_CMD}" -2 "--keep-session-
cookies" )
  WAL_MWLS_CMD=$( append_string_zbksh -1 "${WAL_MWLS_CMD}" -2 "--post-
data='${WAL_ACTION}&${WAL_FORMAT}&${WAL_LGNAME}&${WAL_LGPASS}&${WAL_LGTOKEN}'"
)
  WAL_MWLS_CMD=$( append_string_zbksh -1 "${WAL_MWLS_CMD}" -2 "'${WAL_APIURL}'"
)

  stdout_zbksh "${WAL_WMLS_CMD}"

  (( WAL_PREVIEW == FALSE )) && eval ${WAL_MWLS_CMD}

(( VERBOSE  == TRUE )) && stderr_comment_zbksh -v "${VERBOSE}" -p "Function" -a
"mkWikiLoginSession_zbksh" -d '<'

####
#### Create a login session on the wikimedia server
##################################################
##################################################

(( VERBOSE  == TRUE )) && stderr_comment_zbksh -v "${VERBOSE}" -p "====" -a
"==============" -d '='

#### Loop through each file specified on the command line and upload
#### it to the Mediawiki server, creating a new page or updating an
#### existing page.

  for WAL_FILE in "${@}"
  do

(( VERBOSE  == TRUE )) && stderr_comment_zbksh -v "${VERBOSE}" -p "Function" -a
"wikiAutoLoad"
```

```
(( VERBOSE  == TRUE )) && stderr_comment_zbksh -v "${VERBOSE}" -p "File Name" -
a "${WAL_FILE}"

#### If more than one upload file is specified on the command line,
#### use the file name (minus the extension) as the wikimedia page name.

      (( ${#@} > 1 )) && WAL_PAGETITLE="${WAL_FILE%.@(${WAL_FILEEXTEN})}"
      [[ "_${WAL_PAGETITLE}" == "_" ]] &&
WAL_PAGETITLE="${WAL_FILE%.@(${WAL_FILEEXTEN})}"
      WAL_PAGETITLE="${WAL_PAGETITLE//[._,]/ }"

#### extract the page contents from the file and store contents
#### in a shell variable

      WAL_PAGETEXT=$( sed -e "s/'/\"/g;s/$/\\\r/g" < "${WAL_FILE}" )

print -- "wal_pagetext=${WAL_PAGETEXT}" > /tmp/tmp.out

      (( WAL_CONVERT  == TRUE )) &&
WAL_PAGETEXT="${WAL_PAGETEXT//\</%26%6C%74%3B}"
      (( WAL_CONVERT  == TRUE )) &&
WAL_PAGETEXT="${WAL_PAGETEXT//\>/%26%67%74%3B}"
      (( WAL_PRETAG  == TRUE )) && WAL_PAGETEXT="<PRE>${WAL_PAGETEXT}</PRE>"
      WAL_PAGETEXT="${WAL_PAGETEXT//\&/%26}"

#### Loop through each category specified on the command line and
#### add each category to the page contents.

      IFS=$'.,:;|'
      WAL_CATS=( ${WAL_CATEGORIES} )
      IFS=$' \t\n'

      for WAL_CAT in "${WAL_CATS[@]}"
      do
(( VERBOSE  == TRUE )) && stderr_comment_zbksh -v "${VERBOSE}" -p "========
Category" -a "${WAL_CAT}"
      WAL_PAGETEXT="${WAL_PAGETEXT}"$'\n'"[[Category:${WAL_CAT}]]"
      done

(( VERBOSE  == TRUE )) && stderr_comment_zbksh -v "${VERBOSE}" -p "====" -a
"==============" -d '='

(( VERBOSE  == TRUE )) && stderr_comment_zbksh -v "${VERBOSE}" -p "Function" -a
"wikiAutoLoad"

(( VERBOSE  == TRUE )) && stderr_comment_zbksh -v "${VERBOSE}" -p "====" -a
"==============" -d '='

################################################
################################################
################################################
####
#### Retrieve an "editToken" from the wikimedia server.

(( VERBOSE  == TRUE )) && stderr_comment_zbksh -v "${VERBOSE}" -p "wikiAutoLoad
PAGETITLE" -a "${WAL_PAGETITLE}"

####   getWikiEditToken_zbksh   "${WAL_APIURL}" "${WAL_PAGETITLE}"

(( VERBOSE  == TRUE )) && stderr_comment_zbksh -v "${VERBOSE}" -p "Function" -a
"getWikiEditToken_zbksh" -d '>'

      typeset WAL_TITLES="titles=${WAL_PAGETITLE}"

      typeset WAL_ACTION="action=query"
      typeset WAL_FORMAT="format=xml"
      typeset WAL_PROP="prop=info"
      typeset WAL_INTOKEN="intoken=edit"
      typeset WAL_OUTFILE="${WAL_DD_OUTFILE}/editToken${$}.xml"
      typeset WAL_LOADCOOKIES="${WAL_DD_COOKIES}/editTokenCookies${$}.txt"
      typeset WAL_GWET_CMD="wget --debug --no-check-certificate"
```

```
(( VERBOSE  == TRUE )) && stderr_comment_zbksh -v "${VERBOSE}" -p "Command" -a
"wget ${WAL_APIURL}" -d '>'

        WAL_GWET_CMD="wget --debug --no-check-certificate"
        WAL_GWET_CMD=$( append_string_zbksh -1 "${WAL_GWET_CMD}" -2 "-O
'${WAL_OUTFILE}'" )
        WAL_GWET_CMD=$( append_string_zbksh -1 "${WAL_GWET_CMD}" -2 "--load-
cookies '${WAL_LOADCOOKIES}'" )
        WAL_GWET_CMD=$( append_string_zbksh -1 "${WAL_GWET_CMD}" -2 "--keep-
session-cookies" )
        WAL_GWET_CMD=$( append_string_zbksh -1 "${WAL_GWET_CMD}" -2 "--post-
data='${WAL_ACTION}&${WAL_FORMAT}&${WAL_PROP}&${WAL_TITLES}&${WAL_INTOKEN}'" )
        WAL_GWET_CMD=$( append_string_zbksh -1 "${WAL_GWET_CMD}" -2
"'${WAL_APIURL}'" )

        stdout_zbksh "${WAL_GWET_CMD}"

        (( WAL_PREVIEW == FALSE )) && eval ${WAL_GWET_CMD}

        WAL_EDITTOKEN=$( < "${WAL_OUTFILE}" )
        WAL_EDITTOKEN="${WAL_EDITTOKEN#*edittoken=\"}"
        WAL_EDITTOKEN="${WAL_EDITTOKEN%+*}"
        WAL_EDITTOKEN="${WAL_EDITTOKEN}%2B%5C"

(( VERBOSE  == TRUE )) && stderr_comment_zbksh -v "${VERBOSE}" -p
"getWikiEditToken_zbksh EDITTOKEN" -a "${WAL_EDITTOKEN}" -d '>'

(( VERBOSE  == TRUE )) && stderr_comment_zbksh -v "${VERBOSE}" -p "Function" -a
"getWikiEditToken_zbksh" -d '<'

####
#### Retrieve an "editToken" from the wikimedia server.
################################################
################################################
################################################

(( VERBOSE  == TRUE )) && stderr_comment_zbksh -v "${VERBOSE}" -p "====" -a
"===============" -d '='

################################################
################################################
################################################
####
#### Upload the page contents to the wikimedia Server.

(( VERBOSE  == TRUE )) && stderr_comment_zbksh -v "${VERBOSE}" -p "Function" -a
"wikiAutoLoad"

#### Upload the page contents to the wikimedia Server.

####     editWikiPage_zbksh "${WAL_APIURL}" "${WAL_PAGETITLE}"
"${WAL_PAGETEXT}" "${WAL_EDITTOKEN}" -d '>'

(( VERBOSE  == TRUE )) && stderr_comment_zbksh -v "${VERBOSE}" -p "Function" -a
"editWikiPage_zbksh" -d '>'

        typeset WAL_TITLE="title=${WAL_PAGETITLE}"
#       typeset WAL_TEXT=$( stdout_zbksh "<P>${WAL_PAGETEXT}</P>" | sed -e
's|^$|</P><P>|g' | uniq )
        typeset WAL_TEXT="${WAL_PAGETEXT}"
        typeset WAL_TEXT="text=${WAL_TEXT}"
        typeset WAL_EDITTOKEN="token=${WAL_EDITTOKEN}"

        typeset WAL_ACTION="action=edit"
        typeset WAL_RECREATE="recreate"
        typeset WAL_OUTFILE="${WAL_DD_OUTFILE}/editPage${$}.xml"
        typeset WAL_LOADCOOKIES="${WAL_DD_COOKIES}/editTokenCookies${$}.txt"

(( VERBOSE  == TRUE )) && stderr_comment_zbksh -v "${VERBOSE}" -p
"editWikiPage_zbksh" -a "${WAL_PAGETITLE}" -d '>'

        WAL_EWP_CMD="wget --debug --no-check-certificate"
```

```
        WAL_EWP_CMD=$( append_string_zbksh -1 "${WAL_EWP_CMD}" -2 "-o
'${WAL_OUTFILE}'" )
        WAL_EWP_CMD=$( append_string_zbksh -1 "${WAL_EWP_CMD}" -2 "--load-cookies
'${WAL_LOADCOOKIES}'" )
        WAL_EWP_CMD=$( append_string_zbksh -1 "${WAL_EWP_CMD}" -2 "--post-
data='${WAL_ACTION}&${WAL_TITLE}&${WAL_RECREATE}&${WAL_TEXT}&${WAL_EDITTOKEN}'"
)
        WAL_EWP_CMD=$( append_string_zbksh -1 "${WAL_EWP_CMD}" -2
"'${WAL_APIURL}'" )

        stdout_zbksh "testing = ${WAL_EWP_CMD}"

        (( WAL_PREVIEW == FALSE )) && eval ${WAL_EWP_CMD}

(( VERBOSE  == TRUE )) && stderr_comment_zbksh -v "${VERBOSE}" -p "Function" -a
"editWikiPage_zbksh" -d '<'

####
#### Upload the page contents to the Wikimedia Server.
#################################################
#################################################
#################################################

  done

(( VERBOSE  == TRUE )) && stderr_comment_zbksh -v "${VERBOSE}" -p "====" -a
"==============" -d '='

(( VERBOSE  == TRUE )) && stderr_comment_zbksh -v "${VERBOSE}" -p "Function" -a
"wikiAutoLoad"

#### Remove all temporary output and cookie files
    [[ -f "${WAL_DD_OUTFILE}/wget${$}.out" ]] && rm -f
"${WAL_DD_OUTFILE}/wget${$}.out"
    [[ -f "${WAL_DD_OUTFILE}/loginToken${$}.xml" ]] && rm -f
"${WAL_DD_OUTFILE}/loginToken${$}.xml"
    [[ -f "${WAL_DD_COOKIES}/loginTokenCookies${$}.txt" ]] && rm -f
"${WAL_DD_COOKIES}/loginTokenCookies${$}.txt"
    [[ -f "${WAL_DD_OUTFILE}/wikiLogin${$}.xml" ]] && rm -f
"${WAL_DD_OUTFILE}/wikiLogin${$}.xml"
    [[ -f "${WAL_DD_COOKIES}/editTokenCookies${$}.txt" ]] && rm -f
"${WAL_DD_COOKIES}/editTokenCookies${$}.txt"
    [[ -f "${WAL_DD_OUTFILE}/editToken${$}.xml" ]] && rm -f
"${WAL_DD_OUTFILE}/editToken${$}.xml"
    [[ -f "${WAL_DD_OUTFILE}/editPage${$}.xml" ]] && rm -f
"${WAL_DD_OUTFILE}/editPage${$}.xml"

  return 0
}

####
#### #################################################
```

Appendix E

Function: my_template04_zbksh

```
#!/usr/bin/ksh93
#!/bin/bash
#!/bin/zsh
####################################################
####
#### Description:
####
#### Place a full text description of your shell function here.
####
#### Assumptions:
####
#### Provide a list of assumptions your shell function makes,
#### with a description of each assumption.
####
#### Dependencies:
####
#### Provide a list of dependencies your shell function has,
#### with a description of each dependency.
####
#### Products:
####
#### Provide a list of output your shell function produces,
#### with a description of each product.
####
#### Configured Usage:
####
#### Describe how your shell function should be used.
####
#### Details:
####
#### Place nothing here, the details are your shell function.
####
####################################################
function my_template04_zbksh {

    typeset TRUE="${TRUE:-0}"
    typeset FALSE="${FALSE:-1}"
    typeset VERBOSE="${VERBOSE:-${FALSE}}"
    typeset VERYVERB="${VERYVERB:-${FALSE}}"
    typeset OPTIND="1"
    typeset MYT_PROGRAM="my_template04_zbksh"
    typeset MYT_VERSION="1.0"
    typeset MYT_TGGLEUP="${FALSE}"
    typeset MYT_TGGLELO="${FALSE}"
    typeset MYT_ARGVALU=""
    typeset MYT_OPTIND="${OPTIND:-1}"


####################################################

    find_dot_file_zbksh -f "${MYT_PROGRAM}" -a "configure"

####################################################

#### Process the command line options and arguments.

    OPTIND="1"
    while getopts ":vVulDE" OPTION
    do
        case "${OPTION}" in
            'u') MYT_TGGLEUP="${TRUE}";;
            'l') MYT_TGGLELO="${TRUE}";;
            'v') VERBOSE="${TRUE}";;
```

```
          'V') VERYVERB="${TRUE}";;
          'D') find_dot_file_zbksh -f "${MYT_PROGRAM}" -a "document" && return
4;;
          'E') find_dot_file_zbksh -f "${MYT_PROGRAM}" -a "example"  && return
5;;
          '?') find_dot_file_zbksh -f "${MYT_PROGRAM}" -a "usagemsg" && return
1 ;;
          ':') find_dot_file_zbksh -f "${MYT_PROGRAM}" -a "usagemsg" && return
2 ;;
          '#') find_dot_file_zbksh -f "${MYT_PROGRAM}" -a "usagemsg" && return
3 ;;
      esac
  done

  shift $(( ${OPTIND} - 1 ))

###################################################

#### Place any command line option error checking statements
#### here.  If an error is detected, print a message to
#### standard error, and return from this function with a
#### non-zero return code.

  if (( MYT_TGGLEUP == TRUE )) &&
     (( MYT_TGGLELO == TRUE ))
  then
      stderr_zbksh "# ERROR: Do not specify both upper and lower case
conversion together"
      find_dot_file_zbksh -f "${MYT_PROGRAM}" -a "usagemsg"
      return 11
  fi

###################################################

  (( VERYVERB == TRUE )) && set -x
  (( VERBOSE  == TRUE )) && stderr_zbksh "# Program Name..........:
${MYT_PROGRAM}"
  (( VERBOSE  == TRUE )) && stderr_zbksh "# Version...............:
${MYT_VERSION}"

  for MYT_ARGVALU in "${@}"
  do
      (( VERBOSE  == TRUE )) && stderr_zbksh "# Command Line Arg......:
${MYT_ARGVALU}"
  done

###################################################

####
#### Your shell function should perform its specific work here.
#### All work performed by your shell function should be coded
#### within this section of the function.  This does not mean that
#### your function should be called from here, it means the shell
#### code that performs the work of your function should be
#### incorporated into the body of this function.  This should
#### become your function.
####

  if (( ${#@} > 0 ))
  then
      MYT_MSG="${@}"
  fi

  if [[ "_${MYT_MSG}" != "_" ]]
  then
      (( MYT_TGGLEUP == TRUE )) && typeset -u MYT_MSG="${MYT_MSG}"
      (( MYT_TGGLELO == TRUE )) && typeset -l MYT_MSG="${MYT_MSG}"

      (( VERBOSE  == TRUE )) && stderr_zbksh "# MYT_MSG Variable Value:
${MYT_MSG}"
      stdout_zbksh "${MYT_MSG}"
  fi
```

```
    return 0
}
#################################################
#################################################
#################################################
####
#### Main Body of Script Begins Here
####
#################################################

####
#### Identify the function library directories to search
#### in the FPATH environment variable

FPATH=~/functions/adv_zbksh:~/functions:/usr/local/functions
export FPATH

####
#### Define the values for TRUE and FALSE,
#### In shell think, TRUE is zero (0) and FALSE is non-zero.

TRUE="0"
FALSE="1"

####
#### Extract the "shebang" line from the beginning of the script

read SHEBANG < "${0}"
export SHEBANG

####
#### Test the "shebang" line to determine what shell interpreter is specified

SHCODE="unknown"
[[ "_${SHEBANG}" == _*/ksh* ]] && SHCODE="korn"
[[ "_${SHEBANG}" == _*/bash* ]] && SHCODE="bash"
[[ "_${SHEBANG}" == _*/zsh* ]] && SHCODE="zshell"
export SHCODE

####
#### Modify the shell specific commands and script according to the shell
interpreter

GBL_ECHO="echo -e"
[[ "_${SHCODE}" == "_korn" ]] && GBL_ECHO="print --"
[[ "_${SHCODE}" == "_zshell" ]] && GBL_ECHO="print --" && emulate ksh93
[[ "_${SHCODE}" == "_bash" ]] && shopt -s extglob     # Turn on extended
globbing

####
#### For those shell interpreters that do not directly support function
libraries,
#### cache all the *_zbksh functions found in the FPATH directories.
####

if [[ "_${SHCODE}" == "_zshell" ]] ||
   [[ "_${SHCODE}" == "_bash" ]]
then

#### Loop thru each directory in the FPATH list using a colon (:) delimeter.
#### Process each directory in reverse order to simulate results of
#### searching the FPATH directory.

    IFS=":"
    FDIRS=( ${FPATH} )
    IFS=$' \t\n'

    END=${#FDIRS[@]}
    for (( IDX=END-1; IDX>=0; --IDX ))
    do
        FDIR="${FDIRS[${IDX}]}"
```

```
#### Gather a list of functions ending in *_zbksh from the directory and loop
#### thru each file using a "for" loop.

        for FUNC in ${FDIR}/*_zbksh
        do
####
#### Check each *_zbksh file to see if it starts with a function, if so
#### cache it in the current environment by running it as as a "dot" script.
####
            if head -1 "${FUNC}" 2>/dev/null | egrep 'function|\(\)' >
/dev/null 2>&1
            then
                . "${FUNC}"
            fi
        done
    done

    IFS=$' \t\n'

fi


####
#### Call the script function to begin processing

my_template04_zbksh "${@}"
```

Appendix F

Usage Message: wikiAutoLoad_zbksh

```
Function: wikiAutoLoad_zbksh     Version: 2.0

Multi-Shell Functions - Sort Function

Automatically upload files as page content to a Wiki Server.

Usage: wikiAutoLoad_zbksh [-?vVfzxDE] [-u WikiUserName] [-p WikiUserPassword]
                [-a URL] [-t PageTitle] [-c CookieDir] [-o OutputDir]
                [-C Category:...] [-e FileExension:...]
                FileNamesToUpload...
   Where:
    -u = WikiUser Login name (Default: WikiSysop)
    -p = WikiUser Password (Default: administrator)
    -a = Wiki API URL (Default: http://127.0.0.1/wiki/api.php )
    -t = Page Title (only valid for single file upload) (Default: NULL)
    -c = Directory for storage of HTTP cookies (Default: .)
    -o = Directory for storage of output files (Default: .)
    -C = WikiCategories to assign to each uploaded page (Default: Upload)
    -z = Preview Mode, show steps but do not upload anything (Default: FALSE)
    -e = Delete matching file extension from upload files
         use remaining FileName suffix as the PageTitle
    -f = Insert Preformatted tags around file content (Default: FALSE)
    -x = Convert imbedded HTTP control characters to URL hex codes
    -D = Generate Documentation
    -E = Execute Examples in Usagemsg
    -v = Verbose mode - displays wikiAutoLoad function info
    -V = Very Verbose Mode - debug output displayed
    -? = Help - display this message

Example: wikiAutoLoad -a "http://127.0.0.1/wiki/api.php" -p wikiuser -C
"Category" *.html

Configuration File: ~/.wikiAutoLoad_zbksh.conf
Usage Message File: ~/.wikiAutoLoad_zbksh.usagemsg

Author: Dana French, Copyright 2016, All Rights Reserved

"AutoContent" enabled (Grutatxt)
"Multi-Shell" enabled
"LocalRemote" enabled
```

Function: wikiAutoLoad_zbksh

```
function wikiAutoLoad_zbksh {

#### ###################################################
####
#### Description:
####
#### The purpose of this program is to provide the shell programmer or system
#### administrator with an automated mechanism for uploading documentation
#### and content to a MediaWiki server.  This shell script can be run from
#### any system in an organization to automatically upload information to a
#### centralized wiki documentation server.
####
#### Assumptions:
####
#### It is assumed the content to be uploaded is stored in files on the local
#### system.  Each paged stored in a separate file. It is also assumed the
```

```
#### filename will be used as the Page title on the Wiki.  When the file name
#### is processed by this script, characters such as underscores "_", commas
#### ",", periods ".", dashes "-" are replaced with spaces, and the file
#### extension can be removed via a command line option.  So the user can
#### create files with names such as "My_Wiki_Page_to_Upload.html", and this
#### script will upload this file to a wiki page named "My Wiki Page to
#### Upload".
####
#### Dependencies:
####
#### This script requires the "wget" command to send files and receive
#### cookies from the Wiki Server.
####
#### Unix Utilities:
####      sed
####      rm
####
#### GNU Utilities:
####      wget
####
#### Products:
####
#### This script uploads the contents of a file and creates or updates a
#### Mediwiki pages on a Wiki Server.
####
#### Configured Usage:
####
#### This script can be run from the command line or included in a library
#### and called as a function.  One or more filenames containing content to
#### be uploaded to a Wiki Server must be specified on the command line or an
#### error is generated.
####
#### Page titles for single file uploads can be specified using the "-t"
#### command line option.  This option is only valid if a single file is
#### specified on the command line.
####
#### Bulk Uploads can be performed by specifying more than one filename on
#### the command line.  The page title for each page in a bulk upload will be
#### the filename containing the content.
####
#### Deleting File Extentions from page titles during Bulk file uploads:
#### Multiple file extensions can be specified for the "-e" option by using
#### the pipe "|" delimiter between each file extension.
####
#### Multiple Categories can be specified on the command line as an argument
#### to the "-C" option.  To specify multiple categories, separate each
#### category specified with a comma ",".
####
#### Details:
####
#####################################################

    typeset PROGRAM="wikiAutoLoad_zbksh"
    typeset VERSION="2.0"
    typeset TRUE="0"
    typeset FALSE="1"
    typeset VERBOSE="${FALSE}"
    typeset VERYVERB="${FALSE}"

    typeset WAL_WIKIUSER="WikiSysop"
    typeset WAL_WIKIPASS="abcd1234"
    typeset WAL_APIURL="http://127.0.0.1/wiki/api.php"
    typeset WAL_PAGETITLE=""
    typeset WAL_CATEGORIES="Upload"
    typeset WAL_FILEEXTEN="html"
    typeset WAL_PRETAG="${FALSE}"
    typeset WAL_CONVERT="${FALSE}"

    typeset WAL_PREVIEW="${FALSE}"
    typeset WAL_DD_COOKIES="/home/dfrench/tmp"
    typeset WAL_DD_OUTFILE="/home/dfrench/tmp"
    typeset WAL_WGETOUT="${WAL_DD_OUTFILE}/wget${$}.out"
```

```
####
#### Process the command line options and arguments, saving
#### the values as appropriate.
####

    while getopts ":vvu:p:a:t:c:o:C:e:zfxDE" OPTION
    do
        case "${OPTION}" in
            'u') WAL_WIKIUSER="${OPTARG}";;
            'p') WAL_WIKIPASS="${OPTARG}";;
            'a') WAL_APIURL="${OPTARG}";;
            't') WAL_PAGETITLE="${OPTARG}";;
            'c') WAL_DD_COOKIES="${OPTARG}";;
            'o') WAL_DD_OUTFILE="${OPTARG}";;
            'C') WAL_CATEGORIES="${OPTARG}";;
            'e') WAL_FILEEXTEN="${OPTARG}";;
            'z') WAL_PREVIEW="${TRUE}";;
            'f') WAL_PRETAG="${TRUE}";;
            'x') WAL_CONVERT="${TRUE}";;
            'v') VERBOSE="${TRUE}";;
            'V') VERYVERB="${TRUE}";;
            'D') find_dot_file_zbksh -f "${PROGRAM}" -a "document" && return 4;;
            'E') find_dot_file_zbksh -f "${PROGRAM}" -a "example"  && return 5;;
            '?') find_dot_file_zbksh -f "${PROGRAM}" -a "usagemsg" && return 1 ;;
            ':') find_dot_file_zbksh -f "${PROGRAM}" -a "usagemsg" && return 2 ;;
            '#') find_dot_file_zbksh -f "${PROGRAM}" -a "usagemsg" && return 3 ;;
        esac
    done

    shift $(( ${OPTIND} - 1 ))

    trap "find_dot_file_zbksh -f ${PROGRAM} -a usagemsg" EXIT

    if (( ${#@} == 0 ))
    then
        stderr_comment_zbksh -c "# ERROR: Upload File(s) not specified"
        return 2
    fi

    if (( ${#@} > 1 )) && [[ "_${WAL_PAGETITLE}" != "_" ]]
    then
        stderr_comment_zbksh -c "# WARNING: More than one file was specified on the
command line."
        stderr_comment_zbksh -c "#            As a result the Page title, that was
also specified on"
        stderr_comment_zbksh -c "#            the command line, will not be used."
    fi

    trap "-" EXIT

##################################################

####
#### Display some program info and the command line arguments specified
#### if "VERBOSE" mode was specified.
####

    verbose_comment_zbksh -v "${VERBOSE}" -p "Program Name"     -a "${PROGRAM}"
    verbose_comment_zbksh -v "${VERBOSE}" -p "Version"          -a "
${VERSION}"
    verbose_comment_zbksh -v "${VERBOSE}" -p "True"             -a " ${TRUE}"
    verbose_comment_zbksh -v "${VERBOSE}" -p "False"            -a " ${FALSE}"
    verbose_comment_zbksh -v "${VERBOSE}" -p "WikiUser"         -a "
${WAL_WIKIUSER}"
    verbose_comment_zbksh -v "${VERBOSE}" -p "WikiPass"         -a "
${WAL_WIKIPASS}"
    verbose_comment_zbksh -v "${VERBOSE}" -p "API URL"          -a "
${WAL_APIURL}"
    verbose_comment_zbksh -v "${VERBOSE}" -p "Cookie Dir"       -a "
${WAL_DD_COOKIES}"
```

```
  verbose_comment_zbksh -v "${VERBOSE}" -p "Output Dir"        -a "
${WAL_DD_OUTFILE}"
  verbose_comment_zbksh -v "${VERBOSE}" -p "File Extension"     -a "
${WAL_FILEEXTEN}"

  (( VERBOSE  == TRUE )) && WAL_TORF="TRUE" || WAL_TORF="FALSE"
  verbose_comment_zbksh -v "${VERBOSE}" -p "Verbose Mode"   -a " ${WAL_TORF}"

  (( WAL_PREVIEW  == TRUE )) && WAL_TORF="TRUE" || WAL_TORF="FALSE"
  verbose_comment_zbksh -v "${VERBOSE}" -p "Preview Mode"   -a " ${WAL_TORF}"

  (( WAL_PRETAG   == TRUE )) && WAL_TORF="TRUE" || WAL_TORF="FALSE"
  verbose_comment_zbksh -v "${VERBOSE}" -p "Preformatted"   -a " ${WAL_TORF}"

  (( WAL_CONVERT   == TRUE )) && WAL_TORF="TRUE" || WAL_TORF="FALSE"
  verbose_comment_zbksh -v "${VERBOSE}" -p "Convert Chars"  -a " ${WAL_TORF}"

################################################
(( VERBOSE  == TRUE )) && stderr_comment_zbksh -v "${VERBOSE}" -p "Function"  -
a "wikiAutoLoad"
(( VERBOSE  == TRUE )) && stderr_comment_zbksh -v "${VERBOSE}" -p "====" -a
"===============" -d '='

################################################
################################################
################################################
####
#### Retrieve a login token from the wikimedia server

(( VERBOSE  == TRUE )) && stderr_comment_zbksh -v "${VERBOSE}" -p "Function"  -
a "getWikiLoginToken_zbksh" -d '>'

#### getWikiLoginToken_zbksh  "${WAL_APIURL}" "${WAL_WIKIUSER}"
"${WAL_WIKIPASS}"

  typeset WAL_LGNAME="lgname=${WAL_WIKIUSER}"
  typeset WAL_LGPASS="lgpassword=${WAL_WIKIPASS}"
  typeset WAL_ACTION="action=login"
  typeset WAL_FORMAT="format=xml"
  typeset WAL_OUTFILE="${WAL_DD_OUTFILE}/loginToken${$}.xml"
  typeset WAL_SAVECOOKIES="${WAL_DD_COOKIES}/loginTokenCookies${$}.txt"

(( VERBOSE  == TRUE )) && stderr_comment_zbksh -v "${VERBOSE}" -p "Command" -a
"wget ${WAL_APIURL}" -d '>'

  WAL_GWLT_CMD="wget"
  WAL_GWLT_CMD=$( append_string_zbksh -1 "${WAL_GWLT_CMD}" -2 "-O
'${WAL_OUTFILE}'" )
  WAL_GWLT_CMD=$( append_string_zbksh -1 "${WAL_GWLT_CMD}" -2 "--save-cookies
'${WAL_SAVECOOKIES}'" )
  WAL_GWLT_CMD=$( append_string_zbksh -1 "${WAL_GWLT_CMD}" -2 "--keep-session-
cookies" )
  WAL_GWLT_CMD=$( append_string_zbksh -1 "${WAL_GWLT_CMD}" -2 "--post-
data='${WAL_ACTION}&${WAL_FORMAT}&${WAL_LGNAME}&${WAL_LGPASS}'" )
  WAL_GWLT_CMD=$( append_string_zbksh -1 "${WAL_GWLT_CMD}" -2 "'${WAL_APIURL}'"
)

  stdout_zbksh -- "${WAL_GWLT_CMD}"

  (( WAL_PREVIEW == FALSE )) && eval ${WAL_GWLT_CMD}

  if [[ -r "${WAL_OUTFILE}" ]]
  then
(( VERBOSE  == TRUE )) && stderr_comment_zbksh -v "${VERBOSE}" -p "wget output
file"  -a "${WAL_OUTFILE}" -d '>'
    WAL_LGTOKEN=$( < "${WAL_OUTFILE}" )
    WAL_LGTOKEN="${WAL_LGTOKEN#*token=\"}"
    WAL_LGTOKEN="${WAL_LGTOKEN%\"*}"
  else
(( VERBOSE  == TRUE )) && stderr_comment_zbksh -v "${VERBOSE}" -p "ERROR: wget
output file"  -a "${WAL_OUTFILE}" -d '>'
```

```
      return 10
   fi

(( VERBOSE  == TRUE )) && stderr_comment_zbksh -v "${VERBOSE}" -p
"getWikiLoginToken_zbksh LGTOKEN"  -a "${WAL_LGTOKEN}" -d '>'

(( VERBOSE  == TRUE )) && stderr_comment_zbksh -v "${VERBOSE}" -p "Function"  -
a "getWikiLoginToken_zbksh" -d '<'

####
#### Retrieve a login token from the wikimedia server
################################################
################################################
################################################

(( VERBOSE  == TRUE )) && stderr_comment_zbksh -v "${VERBOSE}" -p "====" -a
"===============" -d '='

################################################
################################################
################################################
####
#### Create a login session on the wikimedia server

(( VERBOSE  == TRUE )) && stderr_comment_zbksh -v "${VERBOSE}" -p "Function"  -
a "wikiAutoLoad"

####  mkWikiLoginSession_zbksh "${WAL_APIURL}" "${WAL_WIKIUSER}"
"${WAL_WIKIPASS}" "${WAL_LGTOKEN}"

(( VERBOSE  == TRUE )) && stderr_comment_zbksh -v "${VERBOSE}" -p "Function" -a
"mkWikiLoginSession_zbksh" -d '>'

   typeset WAL_LGNAME="lgname=${WAL_WIKIUSER}"
   typeset WAL_LGPASS="lgpassword=${WAL_WIKIPASS}"
   typeset WAL_LGTOKEN="lgtoken=${WAL_LGTOKEN}"

   typeset WAL_ACTION="action=login"
   typeset WAL_FORMAT="format=xml"
   typeset WAL_OUTFILE="${WAL_DD_OUTFILE}/wikiLogin${$}.xml"
   typeset WAL_LOADCOOKIES="${WAL_DD_COOKIES}/loginTokenCookies${$}.txt"
   typeset WAL_SAVECOOKIES="${WAL_DD_COOKIES}/editTokenCookies${$}.txt"

(( VERBOSE  == TRUE )) && stderr_comment_zbksh -v "${VERBOSE}" -p
"mkWikiLoginSession" -a "${WAL_WIKIUSER}" -d '>'

(( VERBOSE  == TRUE )) && stderr_comment_zbksh -v "${VERBOSE}" -p "Command" -a
"wget ${WAL_APIURL}" -d '>'

   WAL_MWLS_CMD="wget --debug --no-check-certificate"
   WAL_MWLS_CMD=$( append_string_zbksh -1 "${WAL_MWLS_CMD}" -2 "-O
'${WAL_OUTFILE}'" )
   WAL_MWLS_CMD=$( append_string_zbksh -1 "${WAL_MWLS_CMD}" -2 "--load-cookies
'${WAL_LOADCOOKIES}'" )
   WAL_MWLS_CMD=$( append_string_zbksh -1 "${WAL_MWLS_CMD}" -2 "--save-cookies
'${WAL_SAVECOOKIES}'" )
   WAL_MWLS_CMD=$( append_string_zbksh -1 "${WAL_MWLS_CMD}" -2 "--keep-session-
cookies" )
   WAL_MWLS_CMD=$( append_string_zbksh -1 "${WAL_MWLS_CMD}" -2 "--post-
data='${WAL_ACTION}&${WAL_FORMAT}&${WAL_LGNAME}&${WAL_LGPASS}&${WAL_LGTOKEN}'"
)
   WAL_MWLS_CMD=$( append_string_zbksh -1 "${WAL_MWLS_CMD}" -2 "'${WAL_APIURL}'"
)

   stdout_zbksh "${WAL_WMLS_CMD}"

   (( WAL_PREVIEW == FALSE )) && eval ${WAL_MWLS_CMD}

(( VERBOSE  == TRUE )) && stderr_comment_zbksh -v "${VERBOSE}" -p "Function" -a
"mkWikiLoginSession_zbksh" -d '<'

####
```

```
#### Create a login session on the wikimedia server
##################################################
##################################################
##################################################

(( VERBOSE == TRUE )) && stderr_comment_zbksh -v "${VERBOSE}" -p "====" -a
"================" -d '='

#### Loop through each file specified on the command line and upload
#### it to the Mediawiki server, creating a new page or updating an
#### existing page.

  for WAL_FILE in "${@}"
  do

(( VERBOSE == TRUE )) && stderr_comment_zbksh -v "${VERBOSE}" -p "Function" -a
"wikiAutoLoad"

(( VERBOSE == TRUE )) && stderr_comment_zbksh -v "${VERBOSE}" -p "File Name" -
a "${WAL_FILE}"

#### If more than one upload file is specified on the command line,
#### use the file name (minus the extension) as the wikimedia page name.

     (( ${#@} > 1 )) && WAL_PAGETITLE="${WAL_FILE%.@(${WAL_FILEEXTEN})}"
     [[ "_${WAL_PAGETITLE}" == "_" ]] &&
WAL_PAGETITLE="${WAL_FILE%.@(${WAL_FILEEXTEN})}"
     WAL_PAGETITLE="${WAL_PAGETITLE//[._,]/ }"

#### extract the page contents from the file and store contents
#### in a shell variable

     WAL_PAGETEXT=$( sed -e "s/'/\"/g;s/$/\\\r/g" < "${WAL_FILE}" )

print -- "wal_pagetext=${WAL_PAGETEXT}" > /tmp/tmp.out

     (( WAL_CONVERT == TRUE )) &&
WAL_PAGETEXT="${WAL_PAGETEXT//\</%26%6C%74%3B}"
     (( WAL_CONVERT == TRUE )) &&
WAL_PAGETEXT="${WAL_PAGETEXT//\>/%26%67%74%3B}"
     (( WAL_PRETAG == TRUE )) && WAL_PAGETEXT="<PRE>${WAL_PAGETEXT}</PRE>"
     WAL_PAGETEXT="${WAL_PAGETEXT//\&/%26}"

#### Loop through each category specified on the command line and
#### add each category to the page contents.

     IFS=$'.,:;|'
     WAL_CATS=( ${WAL_CATEGORIES} )
     IFS=$' \t\n'

     for WAL_CAT in "${WAL_CATS[@]}"
     do
(( VERBOSE == TRUE )) && stderr_comment_zbksh -v "${VERBOSE}" -p "========
Category" -a "${WAL_CAT}"
         WAL_PAGETEXT="${WAL_PAGETEXT}"$'\n'"[[Category:${WAL_CAT}]]"
     done

(( VERBOSE == TRUE )) && stderr_comment_zbksh -v "${VERBOSE}" -p "====" -a
"================" -d '='

(( VERBOSE == TRUE )) && stderr_comment_zbksh -v "${VERBOSE}" -p "Function" -a
"wikiAutoLoad"

(( VERBOSE == TRUE )) && stderr_comment_zbksh -v "${VERBOSE}" -p "====" -a
"================" -d '='

##################################################
##################################################
##################################################
####
#### Retrieve an "editToken" from the wikimedia server.
```

```
(( VERBOSE  == TRUE )) && stderr_comment_zbksh -v "${VERBOSE}" -p "wikiAutoLoad
PAGETITLE" -a "${WAL_PAGETITLE}"

####   getWikiEditToken_zbksh   "${WAL_APIURL}" "${WAL_PAGETITLE}"

(( VERBOSE  == TRUE )) && stderr_comment_zbksh -v "${VERBOSE}" -p "Function" -a
"getWikiEditToken_zbksh" -d '>'

      typeset WAL_TITLES="titles=${WAL_PAGETITLE}"

      typeset WAL_ACTION="action=query"
      typeset WAL_FORMAT="format=xml"
      typeset WAL_PROP="prop=info"
      typeset WAL_INTOKEN="intoken=edit"
      typeset WAL_OUTFILE="${WAL_DD_OUTFILE}/editToken${$}.xml"
      typeset WAL_LOADCOOKIES="${WAL_DD_COOKIES}/editTokenCookies${$}.txt"
      typeset WAL_GWET_CMD="wget --debug --no-check-certificate"

(( VERBOSE  == TRUE )) && stderr_comment_zbksh -v "${VERBOSE}" -p "Command" -a
"wget ${WAL_APIURL}" -d '>'

      WAL_GWET_CMD="wget --debug --no-check-certificate"
      WAL_GWET_CMD=$( append_string_zbksh -1 "${WAL_GWET_CMD}" -2 "-o
'${WAL_OUTFILE}'" )
      WAL_GWET_CMD=$( append_string_zbksh -1 "${WAL_GWET_CMD}" -2 "--load-
cookies '${WAL_LOADCOOKIES}'" )
      WAL_GWET_CMD=$( append_string_zbksh -1 "${WAL_GWET_CMD}" -2 "--keep-
session-cookies" )
      WAL_GWET_CMD=$( append_string_zbksh -1 "${WAL_GWET_CMD}" -2 "--post-
data='${WAL_ACTION}&${WAL_FORMAT}&${WAL_PROP}&${WAL_TITLES}&${WAL_INTOKEN}'" )
      WAL_GWET_CMD=$( append_string_zbksh -1 "${WAL_GWET_CMD}" -2
"'${WAL_APIURL}'" )

      stdout_zbksh "${WAL_GWET_CMD}"

      (( WAL_PREVIEW == FALSE )) && eval ${WAL_GWET_CMD}

      WAL_EDITTOKEN=$( < "${WAL_OUTFILE}" )
      WAL_EDITTOKEN="${WAL_EDITTOKEN#*edittoken=\"}"
      WAL_EDITTOKEN="${WAL_EDITTOKEN%+*}"
      WAL_EDITTOKEN="${WAL_EDITTOKEN}%2B%5C"

(( VERBOSE  == TRUE )) && stderr_comment_zbksh -v "${VERBOSE}" -p
"getWikiEditToken_zbksh EDITTOKEN" -a "${WAL_EDITTOKEN}" -d '>'

(( VERBOSE  == TRUE )) && stderr_comment_zbksh -v "${VERBOSE}" -p "Function" -a
"getWikiEditToken_zbksh" -d '<'

####
#### Retrieve an "editToken" from the wikimedia server.
################################################
################################################
################################################

(( VERBOSE  == TRUE )) && stderr_comment_zbksh -v "${VERBOSE}" -p "====" -a
"===============" -d '='

################################################
################################################
################################################
####
#### Upload the page contents to the wikimedia Server.

(( VERBOSE  == TRUE )) && stderr_comment_zbksh -v "${VERBOSE}" -p "Function" -a
"wikiAutoLoad"

#### Upload the page contents to the wikimedia Server.

####    editWikiPage_zbksh "${WAL_APIURL}" "${WAL_PAGETITLE}"
"${WAL_PAGETEXT}" "${WAL_EDITTOKEN}" -d '>'
```

```ksh
(( VERBOSE  == TRUE )) && stderr_comment_zbksh -v "${VERBOSE}" -p "Function" -a
"editWikiPage_zbksh" -d '>'

        typeset WAL_TITLE="title=${WAL_PAGETITLE}"
#        typeset WAL_TEXT=$( stdout_zbksh "<P>${WAL_PAGETEXT}</P>" | sed -e
's|^$|</P><P>|g' | uniq )
        typeset WAL_TEXT="${WAL_PAGETEXT}"
        typeset WAL_TEXT="text=${WAL_TEXT}"
        typeset WAL_EDITTOKEN="token=${WAL_EDITTOKEN}"

        typeset WAL_ACTION="action=edit"
        typeset WAL_RECREATE="recreate"
        typeset WAL_OUTFILE="${WAL_DD_OUTFILE}/editPage${$}.xml"
        typeset WAL_LOADCOOKIES="${WAL_DD_COOKIES}/editTokenCookies${$}.txt"

(( VERBOSE  == TRUE )) && stderr_comment_zbksh -v "${VERBOSE}" -p
"editWikiPage_zbksh" -a "${WAL_PAGETITLE}" -d '>'

        WAL_EWP_CMD="wget --debug --no-check-certificate"
        WAL_EWP_CMD=$( append_string_zbksh -1 "${WAL_EWP_CMD}" -2 "-O
'${WAL_OUTFILE}'" )
        WAL_EWP_CMD=$( append_string_zbksh -1 "${WAL_EWP_CMD}" -2 "--load-cookies
'${WAL_LOADCOOKIES}'" )
        WAL_EWP_CMD=$( append_string_zbksh -1 "${WAL_EWP_CMD}" -2 "--post-
data='${WAL_ACTION}&${WAL_TITLE}&${WAL_RECREATE}&${WAL_TEXT}&${WAL_EDITTOKEN}'"
)
        WAL_EWP_CMD=$( append_string_zbksh -1 "${WAL_EWP_CMD}" -2
"'${WAL_APIURL}'" )

        stdout_zbksh "testing = ${WAL_EWP_CMD}"

        (( WAL_PREVIEW == FALSE )) && eval ${WAL_EWP_CMD}

(( VERBOSE  == TRUE )) && stderr_comment_zbksh -v "${VERBOSE}" -p "Function" -a
"editWikiPage_zbksh" -d '<'

####
#### Upload the page contents to the wikimedia Server.
#################################################
#################################################
#################################################

    done

(( VERBOSE  == TRUE )) && stderr_comment_zbksh -v "${VERBOSE}" -p "====" -a
"=============" -d '='

(( VERBOSE  == TRUE )) && stderr_comment_zbksh -v "${VERBOSE}" -p "Function" -a
"wikiAutoLoad"

#### Remove all temporary output and cookie files
    [[ -f "${WAL_DD_OUTFILE}/wget${$}.out" ]] && rm -f
"${WAL_DD_OUTFILE}/wget${$}.out"
    [[ -f "${WAL_DD_OUTFILE}/loginToken${$}.xml" ]] && rm -f
"${WAL_DD_OUTFILE}/loginToken${$}.xml"
    [[ -f "${WAL_DD_COOKIES}/loginTokenCookies${$}.txt" ]] && rm -f
"${WAL_DD_COOKIES}/loginTokenCookies${$}.txt"
    [[ -f "${WAL_DD_OUTFILE}/wikiLogin${$}.xml" ]] && rm -f
"${WAL_DD_OUTFILE}/wikiLogin${$}.xml"
    [[ -f "${WAL_DD_COOKIES}/editTokenCookies${$}.txt" ]] && rm -f
"${WAL_DD_COOKIES}/editTokenCookies${$}.txt"
    [[ -f "${WAL_DD_OUTFILE}/editToken${$}.xml" ]] && rm -f
"${WAL_DD_OUTFILE}/editToken${$}.xml"
    [[ -f "${WAL_DD_OUTFILE}/editPage${$}.xml" ]] && rm -f
"${WAL_DD_OUTFILE}/editPage${$}.xml"

    return 0
}

####
#### #################################################
```

Appendix G

Standalone Shell Script: my_template05.sh

```
#!/usr/bin/ksh93
#!/bin/bash
#!/bin/zsh
####################################################

####
#### Identify the function library directories to search
#### in the FPATH environment variable

FPATH=~/functions/adv_zbksh:~/functions:/usr/local/functions
export FPATH

####
#### Define the values for TRUE and FALSE,
#### In shell think, TRUE is zero (0) and FALSE is non-zero.

TRUE="0"
FALSE="1"

####
#### Extract the "shebang" line from the beginning of the script

read SHEBANG < "${0}"
export SHEBANG

####
#### Test the "shebang" line to determine what shell interpreter is specified

SHCODE="unknown"
[[ "_${SHEBANG}" == _*/ksh*  ]] && SHCODE="korn"
[[ "_${SHEBANG}" == _*/bash* ]] && SHCODE="bash"
[[ "_${SHEBANG}" == _*/zsh*  ]] && SHCODE="zshell"
export SHCODE

####
#### Modify the shell specific commands and script according to the shell
interpreter

GBL_ECHO="echo -e"
[[ "_${SHCODE}" == "_korn"   ]] && GBL_ECHO="print --"
[[ "_${SHCODE}" == "_zshell" ]] && GBL_ECHO="print --" && emulate ksh93
[[ "_${SHCODE}" == "_bash"   ]] && shopt -s extglob    # Turn on extended
globbing

####
#### For those shell interpreters that do not directly support function
libraries,
#### cache all the *_zbksh functions found in the FPATH directories.
####

if [[ "_${SHCODE}" == "_zshell" ]] ||
   [[ "_${SHCODE}" == "_bash"   ]]
then

#### Loop thru each directory in the FPATH list using a colon (:) delimeter.
#### Process each directory in reverse order to simulate results of
#### searching the FPATH directory.

    IFS=":"
    FDIRS=( ${FPATH} )
    IFS=$' \t\n'
```

```
        END=${#FDIRS[@]}
        for (( IDX=END-1; IDX>=0; --IDX ))
        do
            FDIR="${FDIRS[${IDX}]}"

#### Gather a list of functions ending in *_zbksh from the directory and loop
#### thru each file using a "for"  loop.

            for FUNC in ${FDIR}/*_zbksh
            do
####
#### Check each *_zbksh file to see if it starts with a function, if so
#### cache it in the current environment by running it as as a "dot" script.
####
                if head -1 "${FUNC}" 2>/dev/null | egrep 'function|\(\)' >
/dev/null 2>&1
                then
                    . "${FUNC}"
                fi
            done
        done

    IFS=$' \t\n'

fi


####
#### Call the script function to begin processing

my_template05_zbksh "${@}"
```

Function: my_template05_zbksh

```
function my_template05_zbksh {

###################################################
####
#### Description:
####
#### Place a full text description of your shell function here.
####
#### Assumptions:
####
#### Provide a list of assumptions your shell function makes,
#### with a description of each assumption.
####
#### Dependencies:
####
#### Provide a list of dependencies your shell function has,
#### with a description of each dependency.
####
#### Products:
####
#### Provide a list of output your shell function produces,
#### with a description of each product.
####
#### Configured Usage:
####
#### Describe how your shell function should be used.
####
#### Details:
####
#### Place nothing here, the details are your shell function.
####
###################################################

    typeset TRUE="${TRUE:-0}"
    typeset FALSE="${FALSE:-1}"
```

```
    typeset VERBOSE="${VERBOSE:-${FALSE}}"
    typeset VERYVERB="${VERYVERB:-${FALSE}}"
    typeset OPTIND="1"
    typeset MYT_PROGRAM="my_template05_zbksh"
    typeset MYT_VERSION="1.0"
    typeset MYT_TGGLEUP="${FALSE}"
    typeset MYT_TGGLELO="${FALSE}"
    typeset MYT_ARGVALU=""
    typeset MYT_OPTIND="${OPTIND:-1}"

#################################################

    find_dot_file_zbksh -f "${MYT_PROGRAM}" -a "configure"

#################################################

#### Process the command line options and arguments.

    OPTIND="1"
    while getopts ":vVulDE" OPTION
    do
        case "${OPTION}" in
            'u') MYT_TGGLEUP="${TRUE}";;
            'l') MYT_TGGLELO="${TRUE}";;
            'v') VERBOSE="${TRUE}";;
            'V') VERYVERB="${TRUE}";;
            'D') find_dot_file_zbksh -f "${MYT_PROGRAM}" -a "document" && return
4;;
            'E') find_dot_file_zbksh -f "${MYT_PROGRAM}" -a "example"  && return
5;;
            '?') find_dot_file_zbksh -f "${MYT_PROGRAM}" -a "usagemsg" && return
1 ;;
            ':') find_dot_file_zbksh -f "${MYT_PROGRAM}" -a "usagemsg" && return
2 ;;
            '#') find_dot_file_zbksh -f "${MYT_PROGRAM}" -a "usagemsg" && return
3 ;;
        esac
    done

    shift $(( ${OPTIND} - 1 ))

#################################################

#### Place any command line option error checking statements
#### here.  If an error is detected, print a message to
#### standard error, and return from this function with a
#### non-zero return code.

    if (( MYT_TGGLEUP == TRUE )) &&
       (( MYT_TGGLELO == TRUE ))
    then
        stderr_zbksh "# ERROR: Do not specify both upper and lower case
conversion together"
        find_dot_file_zbksh -f "${MYT_PROGRAM}" -a "usagemsg"
        return 11
    fi

#################################################

    (( VERYVERB == TRUE )) && set -x
    (( VERBOSE  == TRUE )) && stderr_zbksh "# Program Name..........:
${MYT_PROGRAM}"
    (( VERBOSE  == TRUE )) && stderr_zbksh "# Version...............:
${MYT_VERSION}"

    for MYT_ARGVALU in "${@}"
    do
        (( VERBOSE  == TRUE )) && stderr_zbksh "# Command Line Arg......:
${MYT_ARGVALU}"
    done

#################################################
```

```
####
#### Your shell function should perform its specific work here.
#### All work performed by your shell function should be coded
#### within this section of the function.  This does not mean that
#### your function should be called from here, it means the shell
#### code that performs the work of your function should be
#### incorporated into the body of this function.  This should
#### become your function.
####

  if (( ${#@} > 0 ))
  then
      MYT_MSG="${@}"
  fi

  if [[ "_${MYT_MSG}" != "_" ]]
  then
      (( MYT_TGGLEUP == TRUE )) && typeset -u MYT_MSG="${MYT_MSG}"
      (( MYT_TGGLELO == TRUE )) && typeset -l MYT_MSG="${MYT_MSG}"

      (( VERBOSE  == TRUE )) && stderr_zbksh "# MYT_MSG Variable Value:
${MYT_MSG}"
      stdout_zbksh "${MYT_MSG}"
  fi

  return 0
}
#### #################################################
```

Hidden Configuration File: .my_template05_zbksh.conf

```
#################################################
####
#### This is the configuration file for the program "my_template05_zbksh". The
#### values show below are the default values for each configurable variable.
#### If you want to change a value, copy the configuration line, uncomment
#### it, and change the value.
####
#################################################

# MYT_PROGRAM="my_template05_zbksh"

# VERSION="1.0"

MYT_MSG="Hello World!"
```

Usage Message File: .my_template05_zbksh.usagemsg

```
Program: my_template05_zbksh         Version: 1.0

Place a brief description ( < 255 chars ) of your shell
function here.

Usage: my_template05_zbksh [-?vV] [-u] [-l]

  Where:
    -u = Convert command line arguments to upper case
    -l = Convert command line arguments to lower case
    -D = Generate Documentation
    -E = Execute Examples in Usagemsg
    -v = Verbose mode - displays function info
    -V = Very Verbose Mode - debug output displayed
    -? = Help - display this message

Example Usage:
    my_template05_zbksh -v -u
    my_template05_zbksh -v -l
```

Author: Your Name (YourEmail@address.com)

"AutoContent" enabled
"Multi-Shell" enabled

Documentation File: .my_template05_zbksh.document

Program: my_template05_zbksh   Version: 1.0

Place a brief description (< 255 chars) of your shell
function here.

Usage: my_template05_zbksh [-?vV] [-u] [-l]

    where:
      -u = Convert command line arguments to upper case
      -l = Convert command line arguments to lower case
      -D = Generate Documentation
      -E = Execute Examples in Usagemsg
      -v = Verbose mode - displays function info
      -V = Very Verbose Mode - debug output displayed
      -? = Help - display this message

Example Usage:
    my_template05_zbksh -v -u
    my_template05_zbksh -v -l

Author: Your Name (YourEmail@address.com)

"AutoContent" enabled
"Multi-Shell" enabled

Description:

Place a full text description of your shell function here.

Assumptions:

Provide a list of assumptions your shell function makes,
with a description of each assumption.

Dependencies:

Provide a list of dependencies your shell function has,
with a description of each dependency.

Products:

Provide a list of output your shell function produces,
with a description of each product.

Configured Usage:

Describe how your shell function should be used.

Details:

Place nothing here, the details are your shell function.

Process the command line options and arguments.
Place any command line option error checking statements
here. If an error is detected, print a message to
standard error, and return from this function with a
non-zero return code.
Your shell function should perform its specific work here.
All work performed by your shell function should be coded
within this section of the function. This does not mean that
your function should be called from here, it means the shell
code that performs the work of your function should be

incorporated into the body of this function. This should
become your function.

```
#################################################
+ eval my_template05_zbksh -v -u
+ my_template05_zbksh -v -u
# Program Name..........: my_template05_zbksh
# Version...............: 1.0
# MYT_MSG Variable Value: HELLO WORLD!
HELLO WORLD!
+ [[ _korn == _korn ]]
+ eval my_template05_zbksh -v -l
+ my_template05_zbksh -v -l
# Program Name..........: my_template05_zbksh
# Version...............: 1.0
# MYT_MSG Variable Value: hello world!
hello world!
+ [[ _korn == _korn ]]
```

Examples File: .my_template05_zbksh.example

```
+ eval my_template05_zbksh -v -u
+ my_template05_zbksh -v -u
# Program Name..........: my_template05_zbksh
# Version...............: 1.0
# MYT_MSG Variable Value: HELLO WORLD!
HELLO WORLD!
+ [[ _korn == _korn ]]
+ eval my_template05_zbksh -v -l
+ my_template05_zbksh -v -l
# Program Name..........: my_template05_zbksh
# Version...............: 1.0
# MYT_MSG Variable Value: hello world!
hello world!
+ [[ _korn == _korn ]]
```

Standalone Shell Script: adv_template05.sh

```
#!/usr/bin/ksh93
#!/bin/bash
#!/bin/zsh
#################################################

####
#### Extract the "shebang" line from the beginning of the script

read SHEBANG < "${0}"
export SHEBANG

####
#### Identify the function library directories to search
#### in the FPATH environment variable

FPATH=~/functions/adv_zbksh:~/functions:/usr/local/functions
export FPATH

if   [[ -f ./.adv_zbksh.prefix ]]
then      . ./.adv_zbksh.prefix
elif [[ -f ~/.adv_zbksh.prefix ]]
then      . ~/.adv_zbksh.prefix
fi

####
#### Call the script function to begin processing

my_template05_zbksh "${@}"
```

Script Prefix File: .adv_zbksh.prefix

```
####
#### Define the values for TRUE and FALSE,
#### In shell think, TRUE is zero (0) and FALSE is non-zero.

TRUE="0"
FALSE="1"

# ####
# #### Extract the "shebang" line from the beginning of the script
#
# read SHEBANG < "${0}"
# export SHEBANG
#
####
#### Test the "shebang" line to determine what shell interpreter is specified

SHCODE="unknown"
[[ "_${SHEBANG}" == _*/ksh* ]] && SHCODE="korn"
[[ "_${SHEBANG}" == _*/bash* ]] && SHCODE="bash"
[[ "_${SHEBANG}" == _*/zsh* ]] && SHCODE="zshell"
export SHCODE

####
#### Modify the shell specific commands and script according to the shell
interpreter

GBL_ECHO="echo -e"
[[ "_${SHCODE}" == "_korn" ]] && GBL_ECHO="print --"
[[ "_${SHCODE}" == "_zshell" ]] && GBL_ECHO="print --" && emulate ksh93
[[ "_${SHCODE}" == "_bash" ]] && shopt -s extglob    # Turn on extended
globbing

####
#### For those shell interpreters that do not directly support function
libraries,
#### cache all the *_zbksh functions found in the FPATH directories.
####

if [[ "_${SHCODE}" == "_zshell" ]] ||
   [[ "_${SHCODE}" == "_bash" ]]
then

#### Loop thru each directory in the FPATH list using a colon (:) delimiter.
#### Process each directory in reverse order to simulate results of
#### searching the FPATH directory.

    IFS=":"
    FDIRS=( ${FPATH} )
    IFS=$' \t\n'

    END=${#FDIRS[@]}
    for (( IDX=END-1; IDX>=0; --IDX ))
    do
        FDIR="${FDIRS[${IDX}]}"

#### Gather a list of functions ending in *_zbksh from the directory and loop
#### thru each file using a â€œforâ€ loop.

        for FUNC in ${FDIR}/*_zbksh
        do
####
#### Check each *_zbksh file to see if it starts with a function, if so
#### cache it in the current environment by running it as as a "dot" script.
####
            if head -1 "${FUNC}" 2>/dev/null | egrep 'function|\(\)' >
/dev/null 2>&1
            then
                . "${FUNC}"
            fi
```

```
        done
    done

    IFS=$' \t\n'
fi
```

Appendix H

Function: execl_zbksh

```
function execl_zbksh {
#### #############################################

    typeset PROGRAM="execl_zbksh"
    typeset VERSION="1.0"
    typeset TRUE="0"
    typeset FALSE="1"
    typeset VERBOSE="${FALSE}"
    typeset VERYVERB="${FALSE}"
    typeset OPTIND="1"
    typeset OPT_SSH="-o UserKnownHostsFile=/dev/null -o StrictHostKeyChecking=no
-o LogLevel=quiet -o BatchMode=yes -o ConnectTimeout=30"
    typeset CMD_SSH="ssh"
    typeset SSHPORT=22
    typeset SSHUSER="sshuser"
    typeset SSHADDR=""
    typeset RETCODE="99"


#### #############################################

    find_dot_file_zbksh -f "execl_zbksh" -a "configure"

#### #############################################

####
#### Process the command line options and arguments, saving
#### the values as appropriate.
####

    while getopts ":vVDEp:u:a:" OPTION
    do
        case "${OPTION}" in
            'p') SSHPORT="${OPTARG}";;
            'u') SSHUSER="${OPTARG}";;
            'a') SSHADDR="${OPTARG}";;
            'v') VERBOSE="${TRUE}";;
            'V') VERYVERB="${TRUE}";;
            'D') find_dot_file_zbksh -f "${PROGRAM}" -a "document" && return 4;;
            'E') find_dot_file_zbksh -f "${PROGRAM}" -a "example"  && return 5;;
            '?') find_dot_file_zbksh -f "${PROGRAM}" -a "usagemsg" && return 1 ;;
            ':') find_dot_file_zbksh -f "${PROGRAM}" -a "usagemsg" && return 2 ;;
            '#') find_dot_file_zbksh -f "${PROGRAM}" -a "usagemsg" && return 3 ;;
        esac
    done

    shift $(( ${OPTIND} - 1 ))
    [[ "_${1}" == "_--" ]] && shift 1
    [[ "_${1}" == "_--" ]] && shift 1
    [[ "_${1}" == "_--" ]] && shift 1

#### #############################################

####
#### Check the command line arguments to verify they are valid values and that all
#### necessary information was specified.
####

    trap "find_dot_file_zbksh -f execl_zbksh -a usagemsg" EXIT

    if [[ "_${SSHADDR}" != "_" ]] &&
       [[ "_${SSHPORT}" == "_" ]]
```

```
  then
    stderr_zbksh -- "# ERROR: SSH Port not specified"
    return 10
  fi

  if [[ "_${SSHADDR}" != "_" ]] &&
     [[ "_${SSHUSER}" == "_" ]]
  then
    stderr_zbksh -- "# ERROR: SSH User not specified"
    return 11
  fi

  trap "-" EXIT

##################################################

#### Define the command execution mode, either local or remote depending upon
#### the value of the SSHADDR variable. If it contains a remote IP address or
#### hostname, define the execution mode variable. Otherwise it are set to
#### NULL, which means the commands will run locally.

  EXECMODE="${SSHADDR:+${CMD_SSH} ${OPT_SSH} -p ${SSHPORT}
${SSHUSER}@${SSHADDR}}"

  verbose_comment_zbksh -v "${VERBOSE}" -c "${EXECMODE:-eval} \"${@}\""

  ${EXECMODE:-eval} "${@}"
  RETCODE="${?}"

  return ${RETCODE}

}
####
#### ##################################################
```

Hidden Configuration File: .execl_zbksh.conf

```
##################################################
####
#### This is the configuration file for the program "execl_zbksh". The
#### values show below are the default values for each configurable variable.
#### If you want to change a value, copy the configuration line, uncomment
#### it, and change the value.
####
##################################################

# PROGRAM="execl_zbksh"

# VERSION="1.0"

# OPT_SSH="-o UserKnownHostsFile=/dev/null -o StrictHostKeyChecking=no -o
LogLevel=quiet -o BatchMode=yes -o ConnectTimeout=30"

# CMD_SSH="ssh"

# SSHPORT=22

# SSHUSER="sshuser"
```

Hidden Usage Message File: .execl_zbksh.usagemsg

```
Function: execl_zbksh     Version: 1.0

Multi-Shell Functions - Execute a command locally or remote

Usage: execl_zbksh [-?vV] [-p port] [-u username] [-a ipaddress] "cmdstring"
```

```
where:

    -p sshport  = SSH Port Number
    -u username = SSH User Name
    -a ipaddress = Remote IP Address of SSH Target
    -v  = Verbose mode - displays function info
    -V  = Very Verbose Mode - debug output displayed

Example Usage:
    execl_zbksh "date; hostname"

Configuration File: ~/.execl_zbksh.conf
Usage Message File: ~/.execl_zbksh.usagemsg

Author: Dana French, Copyright 2016, All Rights Reserved

"AutoContent" enabled (Grutatxt)
"Multi-Shell" enabled
"LocalRemote" enabled
```

About the Author

The author of this book has worked in the Information Technology industry in a variety of capacities for over 30 years. His experience includes programming in several languages, project management, systems administration, data center management, and business management. With extensive experience in both technical and business management, the author possesses a unique perspective of business continuity.

www.ingramcontent.com/pod-product-compliance
Lightning Source LLC
Chambersburg PA
CBHW021406170526
45164CB00002B/522